The Vegan Virus

Timboslice

Copyright by Timboslice, 2023

All rights reserved. No part of this publication may be reproduced, stored in a retrieval system or transmited in any form or by any means, electronic, mechanical, photocopying, recording or otherwise without the prior permision of the publisher or in accordance with the provisions of the Copyright, Designs and Patents Act 1988 or under the terms of any licence permitting limited copying issued by the Copyright Licensing Angency.

ISBN: 9798864396421

Dedicated to
Deep thinkers &
Future Philosophers

Contents

Introduction 2

PART I

1: Virus or Panacea? 12

2: Ascension into Pop Culture 16

3: Glamorization and Promotion 20

4: Validating and Perpetuating the Lifestyle 24

5: The Rise of Products and Brands 28

6: Fashion and Beauty Shifts 32

7: Virtual Communities 36

8: Global Trends 40

9: Psychological and Social Drivers 44

10: Unmasking the Paradox 48

11: The Claim of Moral Superiority 52

12: Philosophy of Harm 56

13: The Silent Sentience 60

14: Selective Empathy 64

15: Virtue Signaling 68

16: Nutritional Pitfalls 74

17: Capitalism and Veganism 78

18: The Dark Side of Farming 84

PART II

19: Alternative Perspectives on Ethical Eating 92

20: Navigating the Moral and Ethical Gray Areas . . 96

21: Ancestral Agricultural Wisdom 100

22: The Regenerative Future 106

23: How Regenerative Agriculture Works 112

24: Regenerative Nutrition 118

25: Solving Scalability 124

26: Transitioning Agriculture 132

27: Cultivating Consumer Consciousness 136

28: Future Farming 140

29: The Bright Future Ahead 146

The Vegan Virus

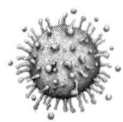

Introduction

As the world becomes more conscious of the impact of our actions on the planet and all living beings, there has been a surge in dietary choices that claim to promote ethical practices and sustainability. Veganism, in particular, has gained immense popularity as a morally superior way of eating. Proponents of this lifestyle often cite animal cruelty and climate change as their primary reasons for abstaining from animal products. However, as we dive deeper into the complexities of veganism, it becomes clear that there is more to this movement than meets the eye. This book aims to shed light on the hidden hypocrisies of veganism and explore alternative solutions that value all life forms.

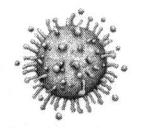

However, this book goes beyond simply criticizing vegans and their beliefs. Its purpose is to encourage critical thinking and questioning the established norms, even if it means challenging our own convictions. We will thoroughly explore both perspectives, enabling us to introspect and contemplate our choices.

See, we all have a lot of growing to do. And it is only through honest and open-minded discussions that we can evolve as a society. So, let us embark on this journey together without preconceived notions or judgments and seek the truth behind the vegan virus.

A bit about me: I grew up as an athletic nerd, passionately pursuing sports and academics. As the salutatorian of my class in high school, I was recognized for my academic achievements. This led me to the University of Georgia, where I was recruited to play baseball while studying Engineering. During college, I experienced a profound inner struggle, wrestling with my beliefs and the intersection of science and faith. This internal conflict gave me a unique perspective on life, constantly seeking to find the delicate balance between reason and spirituality.

Throughout my journey, I have always had a scientific mindset, driven by the desire to uncover definitive proof and answers for everything. As an athlete, I became acutely aware of the impact of diet and nutrition on performance, leading me on a lifelong quest to discover my "perfect" diet. However, as I deepened my faith and grew spiritually, I began to realize that certain aspects of life cannot be fully explained or understood by science alone.

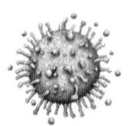

This realization has humbled me and allowed me to embrace a more nuanced perspective on the world. I have come to accept that, as humans, we do not possess all the answers, and it is through this acceptance that I have found a greater sense of peace and contentment. With this mindset, I approach veganism with a curious and open heart, seeking to uncover the truth behind our dietary choices.

I deeply care about this place we call Earth. I care about and love the life I am so lucky to live. Every day, I wake up and crave to make this a better place. This is why I wrote this book. This is why I love tough conversations. This is why I refuse to accept the status quo. We can only bring about genuine change in our world through honest and difficult conversations.

Within this book, there are several of these "tough conversations" that we will explore. This book will journey through many themes and issues, each contributing to a broad and nuanced understanding of our dietary choices and their implications.

Firstly, we will critically examine the vegan ideology, exploring its origins, underlying principles, and potential contradictions and oversights. We will delve into the assumptions it makes about nutritional requirements, environmental sustainability, and ethical living. In doing so, we will scrutinize the potential hypocrisies within veganism while acknowledging its valuable stances against animal cruelty and climate change.

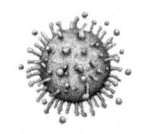

Secondly, we will turn our attention to the environmental and ethical concerns of omnivorous diets, particularly within the context of modern industrial animal agriculture. We will lay bare the grim realities of factory farming, discussing its adverse impacts on animal welfare, biodiversity, and our planet's overall health. Thirdly, we will explore potential solutions that strike a balance between human dietary needs, environmental sustainability, and ethical consciousness. We will discuss regenerative farming as a holistic and sustainable approach to agriculture that values all life, from the soil organisms to the livestock. The dialogue will examine the role of local food systems and the potential benefits of supporting local farmers who prioritize both animal welfare and environmental stewardesses.

Lastly, grounded in the philosophy that all life forms hold equal significance, the book will challenge the moral posturing of dietary choices. We will discuss how respect for all life—from the smallest microbe to the largest mammal—should shape our decisions around food. Overall, the book invites us to consider our relationship with what we eat, challenging us to make conscious choices that respect all life, contribute to environmental sustainability, and still meet our dietary needs. This is not a condemnation of any dietary preference but a call for reflection, dialogue, and perhaps change.

The purpose of this book is not to undermine the genuine intentions of those who adhere to a vegan lifestyle but rather to propose that there may be more to consider in our quest for ethical and sustainable living. It is born out of a desire to delve deeper into these issues, to scrutinize the underlying principles of veganism, and to explore the potential oversights and contradictions within this ideology.

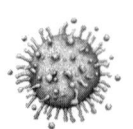

This journey is not meant to incite defensiveness or animosity but to foster understanding and open dialogue. It is a journey into the heart of our food systems, the grey areas between right and wrong, and the complexities of our relationship with the natural world. We begin this exploration not as adversaries but as fellow seekers of truth and co-travelers on a shared journey toward a more sustainable and compassionate world.

Before we begin, I would like to openly share my dietary choices with you, as transparency is essential. My diet is called "Conscious Omnivory," a philosophy that intertwines ethical considerations with nutritional ones, balancing the consumption of responsibly sourced animal products with a diverse array of plant-derived nutrients. This includes grass-fed beef, pasture-raised chicken and eggs, and dairy, ensuring that animal welfare is prioritized and environmental impact is minimized. It eloquently integrates wholesome staples like white rice, potatoes, and wheat, each providing essential energy and dietary fiber. It also engages with the nutritious and culinary benefits of fruits, honey, and nuts, contributing to a varied and vibrant nutritional profile. Herbs and roots like carrots, turmeric, and ginger become crucial components, bringing with them a plethora of health benefits and adding depth and complexity to the flavor profiles of dishes.

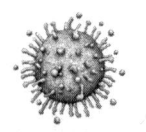

Encompassing not merely a way of eating but a lifestyle, "Conscious Omnivory" seeks to honor and respect all life forms and the environments in which they thrive. The diet posits that ethical eating and nutritional adequacy are not mutually exclusive but can be harmoniously entwined into a sustainable, healthful, and flavorful way of eating. Thus, it unites many beneficial elements from the plant and animal kingdoms, crafting a dietary tapestry that supports well-being, ethical practices, and environmental sustainability. It underscores a compassionate and holistic food, farming, and consumption approach.

I am not perfect, but this has been my attempt to eat responsibly and compassionately. Every day is a chance to take in new information, learn from it, and become a better version of myself.

So, now that you know where I stand, let's dive in. By the end of this journey, you will understand our dietary choices and their implications and perhaps even be inspired to make conscious choices for a better world. Let us begin.

Timboslice

The Vegan Virus

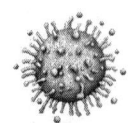

Part 1:
The Virus

The Vegan Virus

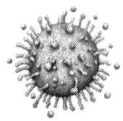

Timboslice

Virus or Panacea?

In the quest for a healthier planet and a more ethical way of life, a movement has risen almost to the status of modern dogma: Veganism. It has become a herald for those seeking to distance themselves from the cruelty and environmental degradation associated with animal agriculture. The motivations behind this movement are noble and reflect a growing concern for more than just our species. However, as with any movement that gains mass appeal, we must scrutinize its efficacy and question its standing as the cure-all for our world's ailments. This chapter aims to deconstruct the vegan ideology, not to diminish its value, but to expose its limits and reveal the more profound solution we need to cultivate.

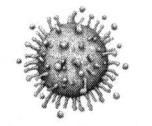

Imagine if we could press a button and reset our food systems – remove every hint of cruelty and environmental harm. Many argue that veganism is that button. But herein lies the crux of the issue: Veganism has been propagated not merely as a lifestyle choice but as an ideological vaccine against the ills of our dietary habits. It has been posited as a virus of sorts – spreading rapidly, mutating into different forms, and suggesting a simplicity in solving complex problems that is, unfortunately, unrealistic.

The Vegan Virus, as it has become, infects public discourse with a black-and-white perspective on agriculture and ethics. It implies a binary choice between right and wrong, good and evil, and in doing so, it undermines the intricate web of dependencies and the myriad of factors at play in our ecosystems. It simplifies the complexities of nutrition, environmental science, and economics into a single, sweeping dietary change. And while simplification can be helpful, it often comes at the expense of deeper understanding.

Firstly, we must address the nutritional aspect of the vegan diet. The argument that it can cater to all human dietary needs is strong; after all, it is possible to live a healthy vegan lifestyle with the correct planning and supplementation. However, this is only a reality for some. Accessibility to a wide variety of plant foods and supplements is not uniform across the globe, and the assumption that it is creates a barrier to genuinely universal solutions.

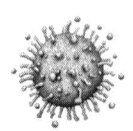

Furthermore, the environmental argument, while compelling, has its challenges. The transportation of often imported vegan foods has a carbon footprint that cannot be ignored. Soy production, commonly touted as a vegan staple, is responsible for significant deforestation and habitat loss. This is not to overshadow the massive environmental issues presented by animal agriculture but to present a fair comparison. We must acknowledge that plant-based agriculture, as it stands today, also plays a role in environmental degradation.

Moreover, the virus analogy extends to how veganism has been absorbed into the fabric of society. For many, it has become a form of identity, a badge of ethical superiority that can divide rather than unite. It prescribes a singular pathway to compassion and sustainability without considering cultural, biological, and socio-economic diversity.

As we delve further into this chapter, we will unpack the limitations of veganism as a singular solution and explore the greater depths of what a truly sustainable and ethical dietary system could look like. It will become clear that the answer to our quest is not found in extremes but in the balance and acknowledgment of the vast spectrum of needs that exist across our global community. Only then can we start to heal the ailments of our food systems and move towards genuine sustainability and compassion.

The Vegan Virus

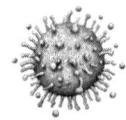

Ascension in Pop Culture

In exploring the ascension of veganism within popular culture, it's critical to recognize its deep historical roots. Far from being a modern invention, the ethos of veganism dates back to ancient Indian and Mediterranean societies, where principles of ahimsa, or non-violence towards animals, were deeply embedded in religious doctrines and everyday practices. These ancient beliefs laid the groundwork for the modern vegan movement, emphasizing compassion and respect for all living beings.

The formalization of veganism, however, is a relatively recent development. In 1944, a British woodworker, Donald Watson, coined the term 'vegan,' distilling it from 'vegetarian' to signify a more extreme rejection of animal products. Watson and his contemporaries established the Vegan Society, championing a lifestyle that altogether eschewed animal exploitation. This marked a pivotal historical moment, crystallizing a scattered set of beliefs and practices into a cohesive and identifiable movement.

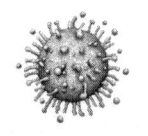

Despite its profound philosophical underpinnings, veganism was initially marginalized and perceived as an extreme or fringe movement. However, in recent years, it has experienced a remarkable surge in popularity, transitioning from a niche lifestyle to a mainstream ethos. This dramatic shift can be attributed to a growing societal awareness of our dietary choices' environmental, ethical, and health implications. People have become increasingly conscious of the impact of their food consumption on their bodies, the planet, and the welfare of animals.

A significant driver of veganism's rise in pop culture has been the endorsement of celebrities, athletes, and influencers. These public figures have adopted the vegan lifestyle and actively promoted it as an aspirational choice, synonymous with health, environmental responsibility, and ethical living. Their personal transformation and advocacy stories have lent a glamorous sheen to veganism, framing it as a desirable and enlightened lifestyle choice.

"Veganuary," an initiative encouraging people to try veganism for the month of January, has played a substantial role in bringing this lifestyle to the masses. It has demystified veganism, showing it as an accessible and feasible option for the average person. The proliferation of plant-based meat and dairy alternatives has further facilitated this transition, with supermarkets and restaurants expanding their vegan offerings, making it easier than ever to adopt a vegan lifestyle.

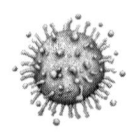

Yet, this mainstreaming of veganism is a double-edged sword. As it becomes more popular, there's a growing concern that its foundational principles are being diluted. The increasing commercialization of veganism, with its market-driven agendas and profit motives, raises questions about the movement's original intent. Is the core philosophy of preventing animal exploitation being overshadowed by marketing strategies and corporate interests? Are we losing sight of veganism's ethical and environmental roots amid the glitz of its pop culture portrayal?

The Vegan Virus

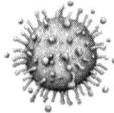

Glamorization and Promotion

The transformation of veganism from an obscure dietary choice to a mainstream movement owes much to the influential roles played by celebrities, athletes, and the media. High-profile figures from the entertainment and sports worlds have not only adopted veganism but have actively championed it, projecting it as a lifestyle choice synonymous with health, environmental consciousness, and ethical living. Their personal stories of transformation and advocacy have significantly shaped public perception, contributing to the allure and appeal of veganism.

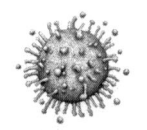

In parallel, the culinary world has witnessed a renaissance in vegan cuisine, thanks to innovative chefs who have successfully challenged and redefined the stereotype of vegan food as bland and restrictive. Culinary artists like Matthew Kenney and Gaz Oakley have been at the forefront of this transformation, showcasing the diversity and richness of vegan cuisine through creative and appetizing recipes. This gastronomic shift has played a vital role in changing the narrative around veganism, demonstrating its potential for gourmet and everyday dining.

Yet, the glamorization of veganism by celebrities and the media is not without its complications. The lifestyle portrayed often reflects a level of privilege that includes access to personal chefs, exclusive vegan products, and nutritionists – amenities that are not readily available to the average individual. This discrepancy raises questions about the practicality and accessibility of adopting a vegan lifestyle for the general population. The celebrity-driven portrayal of veganism, while influential, may thus present a somewhat skewed and idealized image of what being vegan entails.

Furthermore, the media's representation of veganism, though instrumental in raising awareness, sometimes lacks the complexity and nuance the subject demands. Documentaries and news stories often frame veganism as a cure-all solution for various global challenges, from climate change to health crises, potentially oversimplifying the movement and its impacts. While these narratives have been vital in propelling veganism into the limelight, they risk creating oversimplified perceptions of the lifestyle.

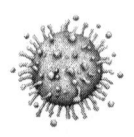

The increasing popularity of veganism, driven by celebrity and media influence, underscores the need for a more nuanced and realistic understanding of the lifestyle. Recognizing the disparities between the idealized versions of veganism and the realities of everyday implementation is crucial. It is essential to strike a balance between celebrating veganism's growing acceptance and remaining mindful of its foundational principles and the practicalities of adopting such a lifestyle. As veganism continues to evolve and integrate into mainstream culture, this balanced perspective becomes ever more critical in ensuring that the movement remains inclusive, accessible, and true to its core values.

The Vegan Virus

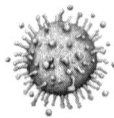

Validating and Perpetuating the Lifestyle

The media's powerful narrative-shaping capabilities have significantly influenced the metamorphosis of veganism from a fringe ideology into a mainstream lifestyle. News outlets have been pivotal in casting veganism as a robust response to some of our time's most pressing global challenges. Environmental crises, ethical concerns surrounding animal rights, and increasing health and nutrition awareness have been at the forefront of this discourse. Documentaries like "Cowspiracy" and "What The Health" have notably stirred public discourse, drawing significant attention to the impacts of dietary choices on health and the environment. However, the portrayal in these mediums often tends toward a binary narrative, depicting veganism as a panacea for environmental degradation and health issues, while casting meat consumption in a decidedly negative light.

In the world of entertainment, veganism has found a new stage. The portrayal of vegan characters in films and

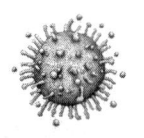

TV shows has significantly contributed to embedding the lifestyle into the fabric of popular culture. These characters are often designed to epitomize virtues like compassion, health-consciousness, and environmental awareness. However, this representation is not without its challenges. The danger lies in the oversimplification and stereotyping of vegan characters, who are sometimes depicted as overly passionate, morally superior, or eccentric. This can contribute to a skewed and often unrealistic image of what it means to be vegan, potentially alienating those who might otherwise have been open to exploring the lifestyle.

The media's influence extends beyond mere representation; it shapes perceptions, molds opinions, and often sets public discussion agendas. While it has played a crucial role in promoting veganism and igniting widespread discussions, it is essential to evaluate these portrayals critically. The journey towards adopting a vegan lifestyle is diverse and multifaceted, varying wildly among individuals. It is not a linear path and certainly not a one-size-fits-all solution. While instrumental in popularizing veganism, the media's portrayal sometimes fails to capture this diversity and complexity.

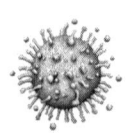

As veganism continues to weave itself into the fabric of societal norms, propelled by its portrayal in the media, it becomes increasingly important to foster a more nuanced and comprehensive understanding of the lifestyle. This calls for a balanced representation that acknowledges not only the benefits of veganism but its challenges and the practicalities involved in adopting such a lifestyle. An accurate depiction is crucial in respecting the complexities of veganism and the individual journeys of those who embrace it.

The narrative around veganism, thus, stands at a crossroads. On the one hand, the media has an undeniable impact in championing veganism as a lifestyle choice. On the other, there is the need for a more grounded and realistic portrayal that acknowledges the nuances and intricacies of living vegan. Moving forward, the goal should be to strike a balance that encourages an informed, inclusive, and empathetic understanding of veganism that respects the choice while recognizing the varied paths and experiences of those who walk it.

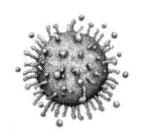

The Vegan Virus

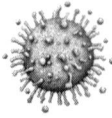

The Rise of Products and Brands

In the evolving narrative of veganism, a crucial chapter has been the burgeoning market of vegan products and brands. The food industry, attuned to shifting consumer trends, has witnessed an upsurge in the development and marketing of vegan alternatives. Global brands and startups have tapped into this market, offering an array of products from plant-based meats to dairy-free cheeses and desserts.

Companies like Impossible Foods and Beyond Meat have made notable strides in creating plant-based meats. These products, engineered to replicate the taste and texture of animal meats, signify a noteworthy advancement in food technology. However, despite their popularity, these alternatives often fall short of delivering the authentic flavors and nutritional value of real meat. They tend to be highly processed and are criticized for their synthetic composition and nutrient profiles that can't match traditional meats' wholesomeness.

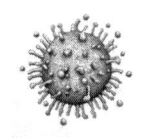

Similarly, dairy alternatives from brands like Oatly and Daiya have expanded options for those pursuing a dairy-free diet. These products aim to emulate the taste and texture of dairy. Yet, they often rely on additives and processing methods that lead to a product far removed from real dairy's nutritional richness and simplicity. While these alternatives have made vegan diets more accessible and varied, there remains a gap in taste, texture, and nutritional value compared to their traditional counterparts.

The proliferation of these vegan products has undeniably democratized veganism, making it a more feasible option for a broader audience. They have helped dispel the notion that veganism is synonymous with dietary restrictions and bland meals, offering convenience and variety to those seeking plant-based options. However, this rise in vegan consumerism also presents a paradox. While these products increase the accessibility of vegan diets, they risk reducing veganism to a consumer trend, detached from its foundational ethos of compassion, environmental sustainability, and health.

Moreover, the nutritional aspect of these products is a growing concern. Many vegan alternatives in the market are laden with artificial ingredients and lack the nutritional integrity found in whole, plant-based foods and traditional animal products. This disparity underscores the need for a more discerning approach from consumers. It calls for a critical assessment of these products, weighing their convenience and taste against the health and ethical implications.

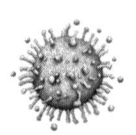

As veganism continues to integrate into mainstream culture, the challenge is to maintain a balance. It is about embracing the convenience and diversity these products bring to the vegan lifestyle while being cognizant of their limitations in terms of nutritional value and their departure from the original principles of veganism.
This chapter underscores the importance of critical consumerism within the vegan movement, advocating for choices that align with vegan ethics and support health and nutritional well-being.

The Vegan Virus

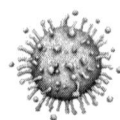

Fashion and Beauty Shifts

The influence of veganism, once largely confined to diet, is increasingly spreading into the realms of fashion and beauty, driven by an ethical consciousness among consumers. However, this shift, while indicative of a growing awareness, is not without its complexities and challenges. Vegan fashion seeks to eschew animal-derived materials such as leather, wool, silk, and fur, aligning with the cruelty-free ethos. High-profile brands like Stella McCartney and Matt & Nat have pioneered this movement, offering alternatives that cater to the ethically minded consumer. However, these alternatives often come with their own set of environmental concerns, such as the use of synthetic materials that are not biodegradable.

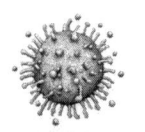

Similarly, the beauty industry has seen a rise in products labeled as cruelty-free and vegan, rejecting animal testing and animal-derived ingredients. Brands like Tarte, Urban Decay, and Cover FX have capitalized on this trend, promoting their products as aligning with a more ethical and conscious lifestyle. However, this shift in the beauty industry sometimes overlooks the complexity of ingredients and production processes, raising questions about the true extent of their environmental impact and ethical credibility.

The commercialization of veganism in fashion and beauty raises concerns beyond the mere absence of animal products. The industry's embrace of veganism is often more a response to consumer demand than a genuine commitment to sustainability or ethical practices. 'Greenwashing' is a significant issue, where companies make overstated claims about their products' environmental or ethical credentials, misleading well-intentioned consumers.

Moreover, the rise of vegan products in these industries often comes at a premium, making them inaccessible to a broader audience and raising questions about the inclusivity of the vegan movement. The focus tends to be on high-end or luxury segments, which does not necessarily translate to widespread change in consumer habits or industry practices. It also reinforces the notion that veganism is exclusive and unattainable for the general population.

Timboslice

The Vegan Virus

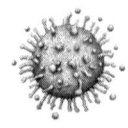

Virtual Communities

The digital era has revolutionized how ideas and lifestyles, including veganism, are shared and disseminated. Social media platforms have become influential amplifiers for vegan communities, providing spaces for sharing, debating, and advocating vegan practices and ideologies. These virtual communities, spanning Facebook groups, Instagram influencers, YouTube channels, and vegan-focused apps, have transformed into dynamic hubs for exchanging ideas, recipes, experiences, and scientific information related to veganism. They play a pivotal role in demystifying veganism, challenging stereotypes, and broadening the understanding of veganism beyond just dietary choices.

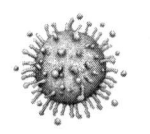

These online platforms offer a wealth of resources and support for individuals exploring veganism. They act as virtual meeting grounds where people from all over the world connect over shared values and interests, offering advice, motivation, and community. This sense of solidarity and collective identity can be empowering, particularly for those who lack support in their immediate social circles.

However, let's examine the less-discussed aspects of these virtual vegan communities. One significant challenge is the development of echo chambers. These platforms can sometimes become insulated spaces where dissenting opinions are drowned out, reinforcing a singular narrative about veganism. This homogeneity can stifle meaningful dialogue and create a binary view of veganism, where it is seen as an all-or-nothing lifestyle, leaving little room for nuance or individual variation.

Additionally, the culture of online discourse, often marked by shaming and 'cancel culture,' can be counterproductive. While aiming to advocate for veganism, these practices can alienate or intimidate those curious about the lifestyle. At times, the aggressive defense of vegan principles overshadows the underlying ethos of compassion and understanding that many vegans espouse. This can deter meaningful engagement and discourage individuals who might otherwise be open to learning about or even adopting aspects of veganism.

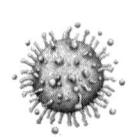

Therefore, while recognizing the value and power of these online vegan communities, it is crucial to advocate for a more inclusive and open-minded approach within these spaces. We must emphasize fostering respectful dialogue, critical thinking, and a welcoming atmosphere in virtual vegan communities. Veganism, in its essence, is about mindful and ethical living. As such, the way it is discussed and promoted online should reflect these values, encouraging thoughtful consideration of our lifestyle choices and their impact on the planet and its inhabitants, rather than creating division or intolerance.

The Vegan Virus

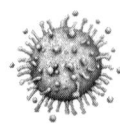

Global Trends

As veganism gains traction worldwide, it presents a kaleidoscope of cultural interpretations and adaptations, painting a multifaceted picture of this growing movement. Vegetarianism has been increasingly commodified in Western societies, particularly in the United States and the United Kingdom. It's often seen as a consumer choice, an ethical statement made through purchasing decisions. This Western interpretation has spurred a burgeoning market of vegan products and brands, transforming veganism into a lifestyle that is as much about what you buy as what you eat.

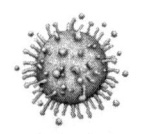

However, the narrative changes significantly when we look at countries like India, where plant-based diets have deep historical and cultural roots. In India, veganism is less about consumerism and more a part of the cultural and religious ethos, where abstaining from animal products is often intertwined with spiritual practices and beliefs. This stark contrast highlights that veganism isn't a modern trend but a longstanding tradition in some parts of the world, seamlessly integrated into the fabric of daily life.

The rise of veganism in Asian countries like Taiwan and Singapore illustrates another facet of this trend. Here, the shift towards plant-based diets is influenced by health consciousness, Buddhist philosophies advocating non-violence, and growing environmental concerns. Veganism in these regions is not just a dietary preference but a holistic approach that blends traditional culinary practices with contemporary vegan principles.

This global perspective on veganism reveals the movement's diverse manifestations across cultures. While in some societies, it's a conscious choice driven by ethical, environmental, or health reasons, in others, it's an intrinsic part of cultural and religious practices. This diversity, however, brings with it complexities in defining and understanding veganism on a global scale.

How veganism is adopted and practiced varies widely and is influenced by various socio-economic, cultural, and geographical factors. This diversity underscores the need for a nuanced approach to discussing and promoting veganism globally. It challenges the notion of veganism as a universal solution or a standardized lifestyle. Instead, it highlights veganism's adaptability and relevance across different cultural contexts.

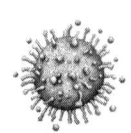

It's crucial to acknowledge and respect these global variations of veganism. Recognizing that veganism can take multiple forms, shaped by local customs, traditions, and needs, is critical to a broader understanding and acceptance of the movement. This approach also calls for a critical evaluation of the Western-centric narrative of veganism, which often dominates global discussions, potentially overshadowing the rich and varied expressions of veganism around the world. In essence, veganism, as a worldwide phenomenon, is not a monolith but a mosaic of practices and beliefs, each adding depth and color to the broader picture.

The Vegan Virus

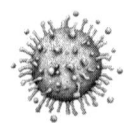

Psychological and Social Drivers

The ascension of veganism can be significantly attributed to the interplay of psychological factors and social dynamics. At its core, the psychological appeal of veganism often lies in the pursuit of ethical congruence. For many, the cognitive dissonance experienced when their actions (consuming animal products) clash with their beliefs (animal welfare) can be a compelling motivator to embrace veganism. This transition is often driven by a deep desire to live in alignment with one's values, particularly in the context of animal rights and environmental conservation.

However, alongside these ethical considerations, self-identity and personal expression are crucial in this shift. In societies where individualism is celebrated, veganism becomes a pronounced way of asserting one's values and beliefs. It serves as a platform for individuals to differentiate themselves, often aligning with broader lifestyle choices that reflect their worldview and ethical stance.

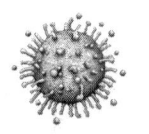

The social aspects of veganism are equally influential. In a hyper-connected digital age, where community and belonging are sought after, veganism offers an entry into a distinct, morally conscious group. The camaraderie and solidarity within vegan communities can be a powerful draw, providing both support and a shared sense of purpose.

Furthermore, the significance of the social capital linked to veganism should not be underestimated. The current trendiness of the lifestyle, propelled by celebrity endorsements and social media influencers, bestows a certain prestige and social admiration on those who adopt it. This social allure, characterized by perceptions of moral superiority and disciplined living, can be a significant driver, especially among younger demographics.

Yet, this analysis brings us to a critical juncture – the need to sift through the layers of social desirability and psychological appeal to uncover the deeper essence of veganism. While positive reinforcement and a sense of belonging are valid aspects of this lifestyle, they should not overshadow the fundamental principles of veganism. True adherence to veganism goes beyond the superficiality of trend-following or seeking social approval. It involves a profound commitment to informed and conscious choices that extend to all aspects of life, not just diet. This commitment encompasses a deep consideration for animal welfare, environmental sustainability, and personal health.

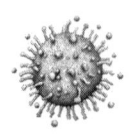

Veganism, in its most authentic form, is a journey of continual learning and growth. It demands more than just dietary changes; it calls for a shift in mindset, lifestyle, and, perhaps most importantly, a re-evaluation of one's relationship with the natural world. This chapter, therefore, seeks to unravel the complexities underlying the psychological and social appeal of veganism, steering the discussion towards a more holistic understanding of what drives individuals towards this lifestyle and what it truly entails beyond the surface-level allure.

The Vegan Virus

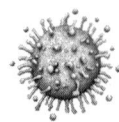

Unmasking the Paradox

The exploration of veganism, often celebrated for its ethical stand on eating and sustainable living, uncovers a landscape riddled with paradoxes and hypocrisies that challenge its perceived moral high ground. While veganism advocates for compassion, fairness, and ecological stewardship, its practices and the narratives woven around it sometimes reveal a dissonance between its ideals and reality.

At its core, veganism is anchored in the principles of non-violence and compassion towards all living beings. Yet, when scrutinized, the commercial aspects of vegan consumerism often stand in stark contrast to these values. The production processes behind many vegan food and fashion products can be riddled with ethical conflicts, such as labor exploitation or environmental harm. This contradiction questions the integrity of veganism as a movement and challenges its claim to moral superiority.

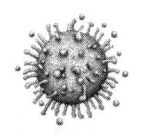

The environmental narrative of veganism primarily focused on reducing animal cruelty, often sidesteps the complex realities of agricultural practices. The shift to large-scale plant-based agriculture, while reducing direct harm to animals, can result in habitat destruction, soil depletion, and loss of biodiversity. This aspect highlights a troubling oversight in the vegan argument, questioning whether its environmental claims fully acknowledge the intricate balance of natural ecosystems.

The health benefits of a vegan diet, often touted as superior, also come under scrutiny. While beneficial in some respects, this one-size-fits-all approach fails to consider individuals' diverse nutritional needs and health conditions. It overlooks the fact that a vegan diet, like any other, requires careful planning to be nutritionally complete and that it may not be suitable for everyone. Additionally, the movement's sometimes elitist and dichotomous stance can alienate those who do not strictly adhere to its principles. This exclusivity fosters a divide rather than promoting a more inclusive understanding of ethical eating practices.

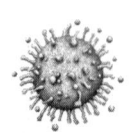

As we delve deeper into the paradoxes within veganism, we aim to provide a candid examination of the movement. The goal of critically analyzing its contradictions and hypocrisies is to foster a more nuanced and comprehensive understanding of veganism. This chapter sets the stage for subsequent discussions on the movement's claims to moral superiority, the subjective philosophy of harm, the overlooked sentience in plant life, selective empathy, and the nuances of virtue signaling. It's about peeling back the layers of veganism to reveal its complexities and ensure that its pursuit aligns with holistic principles of ethics, sustainability, and health.

The Vegan Virus

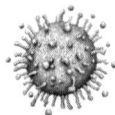

The Claim to Moral Superiority

The notion of moral superiority posits that one's ethical standing is superior to others based on specific actions or beliefs. This belief can manifest in various forms within vegan circles, often portraying veganism as the epitome of ethical living. This section will challenge these claims by examining instances and arguments where veganism is portrayed as ethically superior.

One common argument for the moral superiority of veganism comes from the belief that it is inherently more compassionate. Advocates argue that by choosing not to consume animal products, they stand against the cruelty and exploitation that pervades much of modern farming. This argument is not without merit; the realities of factory farming can indeed be horrifying, and choosing not to partake in such systems aligns with many people's ethical values.

However, the claim to moral superiority here lies in the

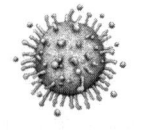

assumption that veganism is the only ethical response to these issues. This perspective overlooks the complexities of our food system and the myriad ways people can and do engage ethically with it. For instance, proponents of regenerative agriculture (which we will talk about in much greater detail later) argue that their practices, which include the ethical treatment of animals, are another viable solution to the problems posed by factory farming.

Another argument for the moral superiority of veganism centers on its environmental impact. In the current large-scale farming system, plant-based diets generally require fewer resources and produce fewer greenhouse gas emissions than diets heavy on animal products. However, this does not automatically confer moral superiority on those who follow a vegan diet. Just because Veganism is better than the current system does not mean there isn't a better solution out there.

Firstly, it's essential to recognize that not all plant-based foods are created equal. Some, like quinoa and avocados, can have significant environmental impacts due to deforestation and excessive water use. Secondly, the ecological argument must often consider socioeconomic factors influencing dietary choices. For many people, access to a wide variety of plant-based foods is a privilege, not a given.

The health benefits of a plant-based diet are often cited as another reason for the moral superiority of veganism. While it's true that a well-planned vegan diet can provide all the necessary nutrients for a healthy life, this doesn't make it morally superior.

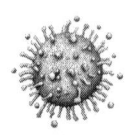

Timboslice

Health is a complex interplay of genetics, environment, lifestyle, and diet. While diet is integral, it's only one piece of the puzzle. Furthermore, the focus on personal health can detract from broader considerations of food justice and sovereignty, which are equally, if not more, important in discussions about ethical eating.

While veganism can be an ethically sound choice, it doesn't automatically confer moral superiority. Our food system is complex, with many ways to engage ethically. As we navigate these complexities, let us remember that mutual respect and understanding are critical to any productive dialogue about ethics and diet.

The Vegan Virus

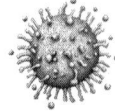

Philosophy of Harm

Central to vegan philosophy is the concept of "ahimsa," or non-violence, which is often interpreted as causing the least harm possible to sentient beings. This principle is derived from Eastern philosophies like Buddhism and Jainism, which are applied universally, not just to dietary choices. In the context of veganism, it manifests in the decision to avoid animal products to prevent the suffering and death of animals for human consumption.

However, the application and interpretation of this principle can be subjective and vary among individuals. Some vegans extend the code to include all aspects of their lives, refusing to use animal-based products in clothing, cosmetics, and more. Others limit it to their diet alone. This discrepancy raises questions about the consistency and universality of the least harm principle within the vegan community.

The principle of least harm hinges on recognizing

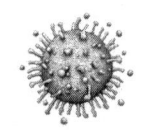

sentience in animals, where sentience is understood as the capacity to feel, perceive, or experience subjectively. While there is scientific consensus that many animals are sentient, the degree and complexity of this sentience are subjects of ongoing debate.

Moreover, the focus on sentience within vegan philosophy can lead to a hierarchy of life where animals are valued over plants due to their ability to feel pain. However, recent research suggests plants also have complex lives, capable of communication and possibly even sensation. If we extend the principle of least harm to all life forms, the line between what is acceptable and unacceptable to consume becomes blurred.

The vegan emphasis on minimizing harm is an admirable goal. Yet, it's essential to recognize that absolute harmlessness is unattainable in our current food system. Even plant-based agriculture involves a degree of harm, be it through habitat destruction, pesticide use, or the unintentional killing of small animals during harvesting. This reality does not invalidate the vegan aim to reduce harm but highlights the complexities involved in ethical eating. A more nuanced approach that acknowledges these complexities and strives for balance rather than absolutes is more practical and sustainable.

Timboslice

The Vegan Virus

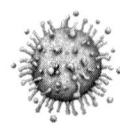

The Silent Sentience

In our exploration of veganism's philosophy, we touched upon the concept of sentience, a central tenet that guides ethical considerations within this lifestyle. Conventionally, the discourse around sentience has been centered on animals, with the ability to feel pain being a key determinant. However, recent scientific advancements have started to shift this narrative, illuminating the fascinating world of plant sentience and perception.

Plants may seem passive, rooted in one place, quietly photosynthesizing. But beneath this calm exterior, they are engaged in a complex dialogue with their environment, perceiving and responding in ways that challenge our traditional understanding of sentience.

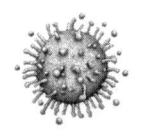

Stefano Mancuso, a leading scientist in plant neurobiology, has been instrumental in uncovering these hidden aspects of plant life[1]. His studies reveal that plants can have complex communication, memory, and recognition behaviors. They can adapt to changing conditions, defend against predators, and warn each other of danger through chemical signals.

Plants have a unique way of communicating with each other. This is primarily done through chemicals released into the air or soil. For instance, when pests attack a plant, they release certain chemicals that signal nearby plants of the potential danger[2]. Upon receiving the signal, these neighboring plants will produce defensive chemicals to deter the pests.

Such intricate communication systems demonstrate an awareness of their surroundings and the ability to respond appropriately, challenging the notion that sentience is exclusive to animals.

Plants are also highly responsive to their environment. They can sense gravity, light, pressure, and even certain chemicals in their surroundings. This ability to perceive allows them to orient their growth towards the sunlight (a phenomenon known as phototropism), to direct their roots towards water and nutrients (gravitropism), and to respond to touch (thigmotropism)[3].

The Venus flytrap provides a striking example of plant perception. This carnivorous plant can detect the presence of an insect on its leaves and respond by snapping shut, trapping the insect for digestion[4].

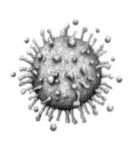

Exploring plant sentience has profound implications for our understanding of life and intelligence. It challenges our anthropocentric view of sentience and invites us to consider a broader, more inclusive definition. Just because plants lack a brain and central nervous system, does that mean they are not sentient, or maybe we don't understand them the same way?

This research underscores the complexity inherent in the least harm principle for veganism. If plants, like animals, can perceive and respond, where does that leave the ethical consumer? As we grapple with these questions, we must remember that our goal should not be absolute harmlessness but a more profound respect and appreciation for all life forms.

Footnotes

1. Mancuso, S., & Viola, A. (2015). Brilliant Green: The Surprising History and Science of Plant Intelligence. Island Press.
2. Heil, M., & Karban, R. (2010). Explaining evolution of plant communication by airborne signals. Trends in Ecology & Evolution, 25(3), 137-144.
3. Braam, J. (2005). In touch: plant responses to mechanical stimuli. New Phytologist, 165(2), 373-389.
4. Böhm, J., Scherzer, S., Krol, E., Kreuzer, I., von Meyer, K., Lorey, C., ... & Hedrich, R. (2016). The Venus flytrap Dionaea muscipula counts prey-induced action potentials to induce sodium uptake. Current Biology, 26(3), 286-295.

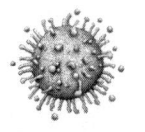

The Vegan Virus

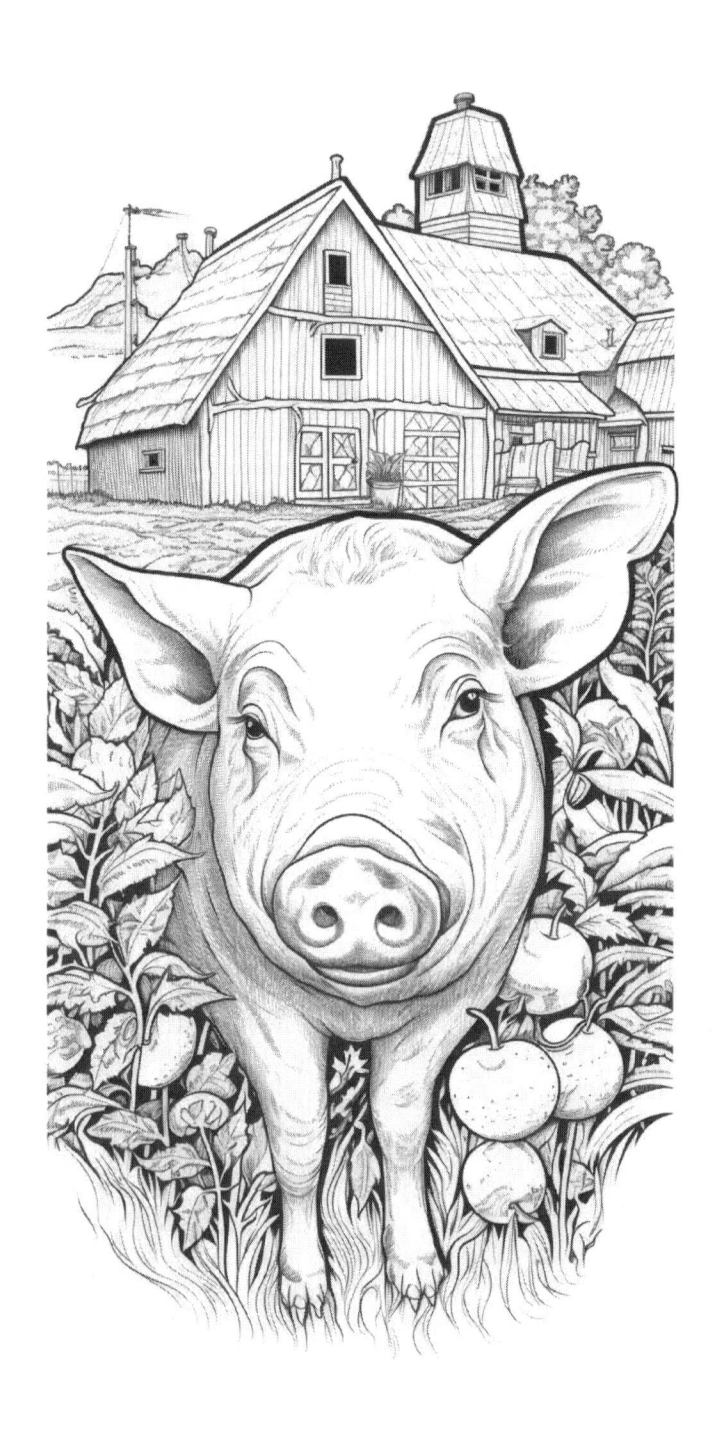

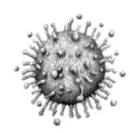

Selective Empathy

The idea of plant sentience now raises some interesting questions about empathy - a key component of vegan philosophy. Specifically, it brings into focus the selectivity of empathy within veganism, where equal consideration is extended to certain life forms (animals) and not others (plants).

Veganism, at its core, is an expression of empathy towards sentient beings. It is a lifestyle choice driven by the desire to minimize harm and suffering. But how do we decide who deserves our empathy? Is it based solely on the ability to feel pain, or are other factors at play?

If sentience is the yardstick, then as we've seen in the previous chapter, plants, too, exhibit a form of sentience. They communicate, respond to their environment, and even display memory-like behaviors. Yet, the empathy extended to animals rarely, if ever, includes plants.

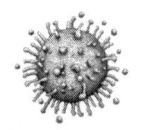

One argument for this discrepancy lies in our ability to relate. Animals, especially mammals, exhibit behaviors and emotions that we can easily recognize and empathize with. On the other hand, plants' ways of experiencing the world are so different from ours that it's hard for us to comprehend, let alone empathize with them.

Another factor influencing our selective empathy is the perception of pain. The ability to feel physical pain is often considered a marker of sentience. Since plants lack a nervous system, the traditional conduit of pain sensation, they are assumed to be incapable of experiencing pain.

However, recent research suggests that plants can respond to damage in ways that are remarkably similar to pain responses in animals. For instance, when a plant is injured, it releases chemicals that signal 'pain' to other parts of the plant, triggering defensive responses[1].

While this doesn't prove that plants feel pain like animals do, it challenges our assumptions about what pain and suffering might look like in different life forms.

So, where does this leave us? If we acknowledge the sentience of plants, should we stop eating altogether to avoid causing harm?

Clearly, there are more viable solutions. What we can do, however, is strive for a more inclusive and nuanced understanding of empathy. One that recognizes the inherent value of all life forms, not just those that resemble us or share our capacity for pain.

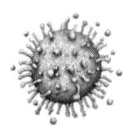

This broader perspective also aligns with the principles of regenerative farming, which respect and value the interconnectedness of all life forms. By nurturing the soil, conserving water, and promoting biodiversity, these practices embody a form of empathy that extends beyond individual species to the entire ecosystem.

Footnotes

1. Toyota, M., Spencer, D., Sawai-Toyota, S., Jiaqi, W., Zhang, T., Koo, A. J., ... & Gilroy, S. (2018). Glutamate triggers long-distance, calcium-based plant defense signaling. Science, 361(6407), 1112-1115.

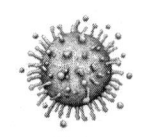

The Vegan Virus

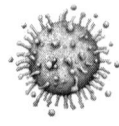

Virtue Signaling

Virtue signaling, a term that has gained popularity in recent years, attempts to demonstrate good character or moral correctness. It's a behavioral display intended to convey a message about one's virtuous qualities or moral stance, often employed to enhance social standing within a group. This phenomenon is rooted in our inherent desire for social approval and is amplified in the age of social media, where moral grandstanding has an extensive platform.

In the context of veganism, virtue signaling can emerge in various forms. It can be seen in the public renunciation of animal products, promoting vegan choices, or vilifying non-vegan practices. Yet, like any complex issue, it operates on both psychological and social fronts, acting as a mirror reflecting our personal beliefs and societal values[1].

From a psychological perspective, virtue signaling

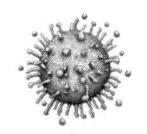

expresses one's moral alignment with animal rights and environmental sustainability. It offers a sense of psychological comfort by helping resolve the cognitive dissonance that arises from loving animals and eating meat.

Cognitive dissonance theory, first proposed by Leon Festinger in the 1950s, suggests that we have an inner drive to hold all our attitudes and behaviors in harmony and avoid disharmony or dissonance. When vegans publicly express their disdain for animal products, they align their actions (not eating meat) with their beliefs (loving animals and caring for the environment). This alignment reduces the discomfort caused by cognitive dissonance, thus providing a sense of psychological relief.

On the social front, virtue signaling enhances personal image and social identity. Being vegan and vocal about it can elevate an individual's social status. They are perceived to make sacrifices for the greater good, embodying self-discipline and advocating for a cause.

Social identity theory, developed by Henri Tajfel and John Turner in the 1970s, posits that individuals strive to maintain or enhance their self-esteem, with positive social identity contributing significantly to this. By adopting a vegan lifestyle and publicly promoting it, individuals are not just embracing a dietary choice but joining a group that stands against animal cruelty and environmental degradation. This membership provides them with a positive social identity and enhances their self-esteem.

One of the significant positive impacts of virtue signaling

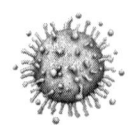

within the vegan movement is its potential to raise awareness. By publicly aligning with veganism, individuals can draw attention to the issues that drive this lifestyle choice - animal cruelty, environmental degradation, and health concerns.

Social media platforms, in particular, have become powerful tools for spreading these messages. Posts showcasing delicious vegan meals or exposing the harsh realities of factory farming can reach vast audiences, inspiring curiosity, empathy, and even change[2].

Moreover, by presenting veganism as a desirable and ethical lifestyle, virtue signaling can help normalize plant-based diets. This can contribute to more significant shifts in societal attitudes and behaviors, pushing veganism from the fringes into the mainstream.

Despite these positive influences, virtue signaling can also have negative impacts on the vegan movement. One of the main risks is the potential alienation of non-vegans. Virtue signaling can sometimes come across as moral superiority, creating divisions between vegans and non-vegans. This 'us' vs 'them' mentality can be counterproductive, driving away potential allies instead of inviting them into the conversation[3].

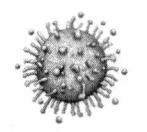

Another risk is the misrepresentation of vegan ethics. While many vegans are driven by a deep concern for animal welfare and the environment, the focus on public displays of virtue can sometimes overshadow these motivations. Veganism can become more about appearing ethical than engaging with moral issues. This can lead to a form of 'token' veganism, where individuals adopt the label without fully embracing the principles behind it[4]. Such superficial engagement can dilute the power of the vegan movement, reducing it to a trend rather than a meaningful response to pressing ethical issues.

While virtue signaling poses challenges to the vegan movement, it also offers opportunities for growth and introspection. By recognizing and addressing these issues, the vegan community can strive for a more authentic and inclusive movement.

This might involve fostering open and respectful dialogues with non-vegans, focusing on common ground rather than differences. It could also mean promoting a more holistic understanding of vegan ethics, one that values sincere engagement over public displays of virtue.

Footnotes

1. Darwall, S. (2006). The Second-Person Standpoint: Morality, Respect, and Accountability. Harvard University Press.
2. Caracciolo, F., & Sobal, J. (2016). Constructing a public eating identity: An ethnography of vegans in an online community. Food, Culture & Society, 19(4), 579-601.
3. Povey, R., Wellens, B., & Conner, M. (2001). Attitudes towards following meat, vegetarian and vegan diets: an examination of the role of ambivalence. Appetite, 37(1), 15-26.
4. Cherry, E. (2006). Veganism as a Cultural Movement: A Relational Approach. Social Movement Studies, 5(2), 155-170.

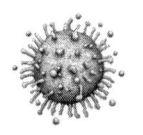

The Vegan Virus

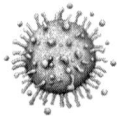

Nutritional Pitfalls

One of the most common concerns surrounding vegan diets is protein intake. However, numerous plant-based foods are rich in protein, including lentils, chickpeas, tofu, tempeh, seitan, quinoa, and various nuts and seeds[1].

The challenge lies not in the quantity of protein but in its quality. Animal proteins are 'complete,' meaning they contain all nine essential amino acids our bodies need. Most plant proteins, on the other hand, are 'incomplete,' lacking one or more essential amino acids[2]. Vegans can overcome this hurdle by consuming a variety of plant proteins to ensure a full spectrum of amino acids.

Vegan diets can be rich in certain micronutrients, such as dietary fiber, antioxidants, and vitamins C and E[3]. However, they may lack others, like vitamin B12, iron, calcium, iodine, and omega-3 fatty acids[4].

Vitamin B12, crucial for nerve function and the production

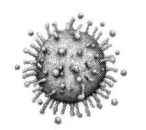

of red blood cells, is particularly problematic as it's almost exclusively found in animal products[5]. Vegans must rely on fortified foods or supplements to meet their B12 needs. Recent research has debunked the long-held belief that algae and spirulina are reliable sources of vitamin B12. Studies have shown that the form of B12 present in these substances is pseudovitamin B12, an inactive analog not usable by the human body[6].

Iron, too, can be a concern. While plant foods like lentils and spinach contain iron, it's in a form (non-heme) that's less bioavailable than the heme iron found in animal products[7]. Consuming iron-rich plant foods alongside vitamin C-rich foods can enhance absorption.

Dietary diversity is key to a healthy vegan diet. Eating a wide variety of foods helps ensure an adequate intake of different nutrients and reduces the risk of deficiencies. The rising popularity of processed vegan foods also poses a challenge to dietary diversity. These products often lack the nutritional profile of whole plant foods and can lead to a reliance on a narrow range of food sources.

While vegan diets can offer numerous health benefits, they also require careful planning to avoid potential nutritional pitfalls. By understanding these factors, individuals can make informed decisions about their dietary choices, balancing the ethical motivations behind veganism with the practical considerations of nutrition.

Footnotes

1. "The 17 Best Protein Sources for Vegans and Vegetarians," Healthline, Aug 2016, https://www.healthline.com/nutrition/protein-for-vegans-vegetarians
2. "Protein in diet," MedlinePlus, U.S. National Library of Medicine, https://medlineplus.gov/ency/article/002467.htm
3. "Vegan diets: practical advice for athletes and exercisers," Journal of the International Society of Sports Nutrition, Sep 2017, https://jissn.biomedcentral.com/articles/10.1186/s12970-017-0192-9
4. "Health effects of vegan diets," The American Journal of Clinical Nutrition, May 2009, https://academic.oup.com/ajcn/article/89/5/1627S/4596952
5. "Vitamin B12," National Institutes of Health, https://ods.od.nih.gov/factsheets/VitaminB12-Consumer/
6. "Spirulina, Vitamin B12, and Blue Green Algae: The Facts," Acupuncture & Nutrition, https://acupuncturenutrition.com/spirulina-blue-green-algae-b12/
7. "Iron," National Institutes of Health, https://ods.od.nih.gov/factsheets/Iron-HealthProfessional/

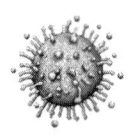

The Vegan Virus

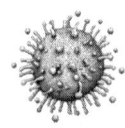

Capitalism and Veganism

The rise of veganism has been accompanied by a surge in the production of vegan alternatives, primarily driven by capitalistic forces. Capitalism's fundamental principle, supply meeting demand, has fueled vegan alternatives' rapid growth and availability. As consciousness about health, animal welfare, and sustainability has grown, so too has the appetite for vegan products[1]. This has led to an explosion in the variety and availability of vegan alternatives in supermarkets, restaurants, and online stores globally. From plant-based meats to dairy-free milk and vegan cosmetics, the global vegan product market is projected to reach $31.4 billion by 2026[2].

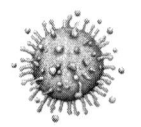

My sentiments regarding capitalism are indeed complex. On one side of the coin, there's a certain elegance to its simplicity. The market is a grand stage where the people speak with their wallets. Consumer demand is the script that guides production; the public's desires shape the landscape of goods and services available. This aspect of capitalism, this freedom to choose and to influence, is undeniably appealing.

Yet, on the flip side, I see the inherent flaws of this system. Capitalism can perpetuate vicious cycles, as it bows to the demands of the many, regardless of the consequences. There is no intrinsic moral compass in this economic model that considers the ethical implications or the long-term effects of these demands. Just because a product is desired does not mean it should be produced and sold without scrutiny. This is where capitalism stumbles. It becomes a question of whether the relentless pursuit of profit should overpower the need for responsibility, sustainability, and ethical considerations.

The burgeoning demand for vegan products has reshaped global trade dynamics. Countries renowned for their agricultural prowess, like the United States and Brazil, are now significant exporters of plant-based proteins[3]. Simultaneously, nations traditionally reliant on livestock farming adjust their agricultural strategies to meet the changing demand.

The vegan market boom has diverse impacts on local economies. On one hand, it creates new business opportunities and jobs in plant-based food production. However, regions heavily dependent on animal agriculture face economic challenges as they navigate this transition[4].

While the growing vegan market offers diverse choices, it often comes with a 'green premium.' Vegan substitutes tend to be more expensive than their non-vegan

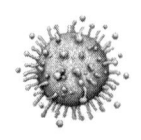

counterparts, making them less accessible for low-income consumers[5]. Addressing this economic disparity is crucial to making veganism more equitable and inclusive.
The capitalist drive has also spurred innovation in the vegan market. Massive investments have been funneled into creating vegan alternatives that closely mimic the taste, texture, and nutritional profile of animal products[6]. These innovations have made transitioning to veganism easier for many, further driving demand.

However, capitalism's role in the vegan movement is not without its pitfalls. The commodification of veganism can lead to a dilution of its ethical origins. Veganism is increasingly marketed as a lifestyle choice rather than a moral stance against animal cruelty and environmental degradation[7].

Moreover, the rise of 'greenwashing' – the practice of making misleading or unsubstantiated claims about the environmental benefits of a product – is a significant concern[8]. Some companies exploit the growing demand for eco-friendly products, labeling their offerings as 'vegan' or 'sustainable' without substantially changing their production processes.

Capitalism plays a complex role in the proliferation of vegan alternatives. While it has undoubtedly increased the availability and variety of vegan products, it poses significant challenges. As consumers, we must navigate this landscape critically, questioning marketing claims and making informed choices that align with our ethical stances.

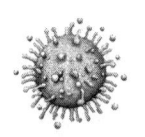

Footnotes

1. "Plant-Based Profits: Investment in Vegan Ventures Skyrockets," Forbes, January 2021, https://www.forbes.com/sites/maggiemcgrath/2021/01/25/plant-based-profits-investment-in-vegan-ventures-skyrockets/

2. "Vegan Food Market Size, Share & Trends Analysis Report By Product (Dairy Alternatives, Meat Substitutes), By Distribution Channel (Online, Offline), By Region, And Segment Forecasts, 2019 - 2025," Grand View Research, Aug 2019, https://www.grandviewresearch.com/industry-analysis/vegan-food-market

3. "The Global Plant Protein Market: What Manufacturers Need to Know," Food Ingredients First, Feb 2020, https://www.foodingredientsfirst.com/news/the-global-plant-protein-market-what-manufacturers-need-to-know.html

4. "The Economic Impact of Veganism," Medium, Nov 2018, https://medium.com/@josephpoore/the-economic-impact-of-veganism-6ee0a4e93b7d

5. "Why is vegan food so expensive?" BBC Good Food, Jan 2020, https://www.bbcgoodfood.com/howto/guide/why-vegan-food-so-expensive

6. "Investors are Pouring Money Into Vegan Startups," The Wall Street Journal, July 2020, https://www.wsj.com/articles/investors-are-pouring-money-into-vegan-startups-11595428600

7. "The Commodification of Veganism," Medium, March 2019, https://medium.com/@jalakoisolomon/the-commodification-of-veganism-7fb74e63a1e3

8. "Greenwashing in Cosmetics. The Brands Doing it May Surprise You," HuffPost, October 2016, https://www.huffpost.com/entry/greenwashing-cosmetics_b_4490045

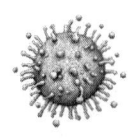

Timboslice

The Vegan Virus

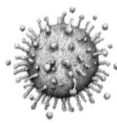

The Dark Side of Farming

Capitalism, in its essence, is a double-edged sword, and its implications on our farming practices are a testament to this paradox. One cannot deny the role of the capitalist pursuit of profits in shaping the current landscape of industrial farming. As economic interests overpowered ethical considerations, our agricultural methods took a dangerous detour, hazardous to the planet and the myriad of life forms it supports.

Industrial farming, with its mechanized cultivation and intensive livestock rearing, is a direct outcome of this capitalistic influence. It is a product of the relentless quest for higher yields, expedited production, and increased profits. But as we chase these economic gains, we often disregard the significant environmental costs associated with such practices.

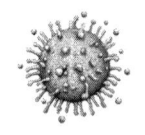

Therein lies the dark side of farming. The excessive use of synthetic fertilizers and pesticides, the cruel confinement of animals in factory farms, and the massive deforestation for agricultural expansion - these practices have wreaked havoc on our ecosystems. They've resulted in the loss of biodiversity, triggered alarming rates of soil erosion, polluted our water bodies, and contributed significantly to global climate change.

Our choices at the grocery store are votes cast for the type of world we want to live in. It is high time we rethink the role of capitalism in our food systems and consider more ethical, sustainable, and regenerative ways of farming. We have examined the capitalistic forces driving the proliferation of vegan alternatives. Now, we must shift our focus to a significant contributing factor to the rise of veganism: the negative impacts of industrial animal farming.

Industrial animal farming, often called factory farming, has been widely criticized for its treatment of animals. Living conditions in these facilities are often cramped, with animals given little room to move or behave naturally[1]. These conditions, coupled with practices such as tail docking, debeaking, and early weaning, raise serious animal welfare concerns.

Industrial animal farming also inflicts severe damage to the environment. The massive amounts of manure these operations produce can contaminate water supplies, harm wildlife, and degrade natural ecosystems[2]. Additionally, the overuse of antibiotics in factory farming can lead to antibiotic resistance, a pressing public health concern[3].

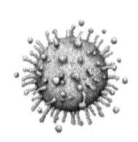

Perhaps most alarming is the significant role industrial animal farming plays in climate change. Livestock farming contributes to around 14.5% of global greenhouse gas emissions, more than all transportation combined[4]. It is also a leading driver of deforestation, as vast tracts of forest are cleared to create pastureland and grow feed crops.

The plant-based side of industrial agriculture is not so pretty either. Monocrop agriculture, the practice of growing a single crop year after year on the same land, can lead to severe soil degradation. Repeatedly planting the same crop depletes the soil of specific nutrients, leading to a decline in soil fertility over time[5]. This degradation threatens long-term food security and contributes to climate change through the release of stored carbon.

Monocrop agriculture also contributes significantly to the loss of biodiversity. Natural ecosystems are often cleared to make way for vast monocrop fields, destroying habitats and disrupting local species[6]. Additionally, the lack of crop diversity can lead to increased pests and diseases, further threatening biodiversity both within and beyond the field.

Farmers often resort to heavy pesticide usage to combat the increased susceptibility to pests and diseases that come with monoculture. These chemicals can have devastating effects on non-target organisms and contaminate water sources, posing risks to wildlife, human health, and the environment[7].

In conclusion, while plant-based diets have been

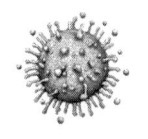

championed for their environmental benefits, it's crucial to consider the potential harm of the agricultural practices behind our food. As we critique veganism and explore alternatives, we must push for more sustainable and diverse agricultural practices that respect and nurture our planet.

Footnotes

1. "Farm Animal Welfare," ASPCA, https://www.aspca.org/animal-cruelty/farm-animal-welfare
2. "Pollution from Giant Livestock Farms Threatens Public Health," NRDC, August 2001, https://www.nrdc.org/issues/pollution-giant-livestock-farms-threatens-public-health
3. "Antibiotic Resistance from the Farm to the Table," CDC, May 2020, https://www.cdc.gov/foodsafety/challenges/from-farm-to-table.html
4. "Tackling Climate Change through Livestock," FAO, 2013, http://www.fao.org/3/i3437e/i3437e.pdf
5. "Soil Degradation, Land Scarcity and Food Security: Reviewing a Complex Challenge," Sustainability, March 2016, https://www.mdpi.com/2071-1050/8/3/281
6. "Monoculture and the Collapse of Global Biodiversity," The Balance, June 2021, https://www.thebalance.com/monoculture-crops-5190927
7. "Impacts of Pesticides on Human Health and the Environment," Journal of Toxicology and Environmental Health, July 2020, https://www.tandfonline.com/doi/full/10.1080/10937404.2020.1791675

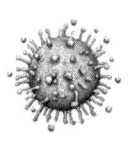

The Vegan Virus

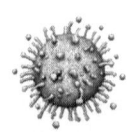

Part 2:
Finding the Cure

The Vegan Virus

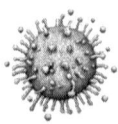

Alternate Perspectives on Ethical Eating

As we've explored the nuances of the vegan movement, it's important to consider that veganism isn't the only dietary practice rooted in ethics. Other movements, such as locavorism and conscious omnivorism, also claim an ethical basis for their choices.

Locavorism describes the practice of buying and consuming food grown within a certain radius of where one lives, commonly defined as 100 miles[1]. The idea is to minimize the environmental impact of food transportation, support local economies, and promote fresher, seasonal eating.

Locavores lionize local foods and oppose food transported over long distances[2]. This movement could reduce greenhouse gas emissions associated with food miles and support biodiversity through small-scale, diversified farming practices.

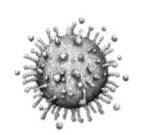

However, like veganism, locavorism can be critiqued as elitist, mainly when local foods are more expensive or less accessible than imported ones[3]. Also, focusing solely on food miles can overlook other significant environmental impacts, such as water usage and farming practices.

Conscious omnivorism, on the other hand, involves a purposeful choice to consume a balanced diet of both plant and animal products, sourced ethically and sustainably. It's grounded in the belief that all life forms are significant and interconnected and that ethical consumption should consider the welfare of animals, plants, and the environment.

Conscious omnivores might choose grass-fed beef over factory-farmed meat, or locally-grown organic produce over imported conventional fruits and vegetables. They advocate for humane animal farming practices and support regenerative farming methods that enhance soil health and biodiversity.

However, like veganism and locavorism, conscious omnivorism is subject to critique over accessibility, affordability, and the varying definitions of 'ethical' and 'sustainable' in food production.

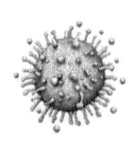

While these movements differ in their dietary prescriptions, they share a common thread: a commitment to ethical consumption. Veganism emphasizes animal welfare and environmental sustainability, locavorism prioritizes local economies and reduced food miles, and conscious omnivorism champions humane animal farming and ecological balance.

However, each approach also has its limitations. Veganism can overlook plant sentience and the potential benefits of animal-inclusive regenerative farming. Locavorism can neglect the broader environmental impacts of food production. And conscious omnivorism requires careful sourcing and constant vigilance to ensure ethical standards are met.

While there's no one-size-fits-all solution to ethical eating, exploring these diverse perspectives can help us navigate our food choices with greater awareness, empathy, and respect for all life forms.

Footnotes

1. "Locavorism: Elitist food snobbery or practical solution to global warming," DownToEarth, March 2010, https://www.downtoearth.org/blogs/2010-03/locavorism-elitist-food-snobbery-or-practical-solution-to-global-warming
2. "Understanding local food consumption from an ideological perspective," Journal of Retailing and Consumer Services, 2021, https://www.sciencedirect.com/science/article/abs/pii/S0969698920313382
3. "Locavorism: A Primer," Paste Magazine, https://www.pastemagazine.com/food/diet/local-food-farmers-markets-locavorism-primer/.

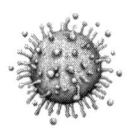

The Vegan Virus

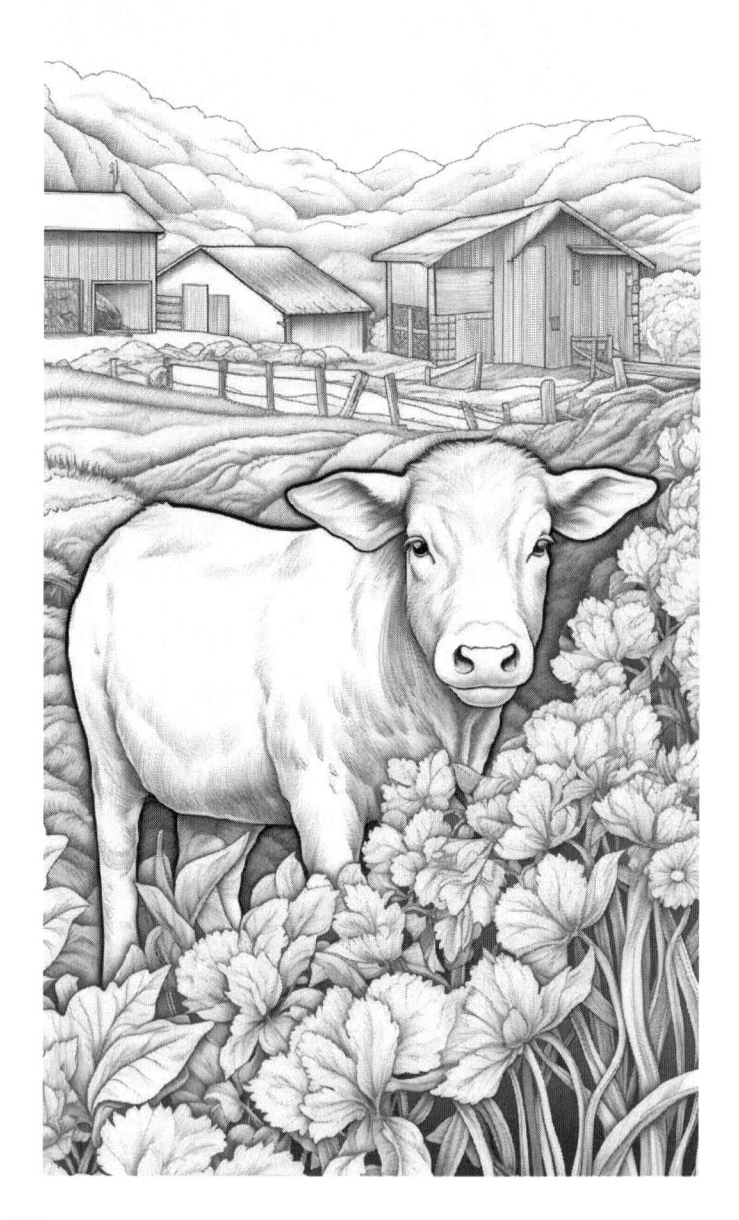

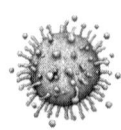

Navigating the Moral and Ethical Gray Areas

Now, it's become clear that the ethics of dietary choices are far from black and white. Regardless of the path we choose, navigating the moral and ethical landscape of what we eat is fraught with complexities and contradictions.

The quest for ethical eating is a journey through a labyrinth of considerations. We must weigh the welfare of animals against the rights of plants, the environmental impact of food production against its socioeconomic consequences, and our health needs against the ethical implications of our diet.

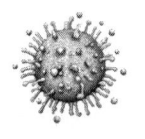

For example, a vegan might choose plant-based foods to minimize animal suffering, but in doing so, it could contribute to the exploitation of human labor in agricultural industries[1]. A locavore might support local farmers but inadvertently promote monoculture farming practices that harm biodiversity. While striving for a balanced diet, a conscious omnivore might struggle to find truly ethically sourced animal products.

These examples highlight the multi-faceted nature of dietary ethics. Each choice we make has a ripple effect, touching on countless other issues that extend far beyond our plates.

In addition to their complexity, the ethics of dietary choices are also characterized by inherent contradictions. For instance, a perfectly ethical diet in one context might be highly unethical in another.

Consider a person living in the Arctic Circle, where plant-based foods are scarce for much of the year. In this context, a diet rich in hunted or fished animal products might be the most sustainable and ethical option[2]. Yet, in a different geographical context, with access to diverse plant-based foods, the same diet could be considered environmentally destructive and ethically questionable. This highlights a fundamental truth about dietary ethics: they are context-dependent. In one situation, what is ethical for one person may differ from another.

Given these complexities and contradictions, how can we navigate the gray areas of dietary ethics? One approach might be to embrace a flexible and context-sensitive perspective, recognizing that there is no 'one-size-fits-all' answer to ethical eating. This might involve adopting principles from various dietary philosophies based on our unique circumstances and values.

Ultimately, navigating the gray areas of dietary ethics

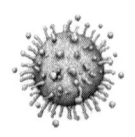

requires humility, openness, and a willingness to learn and adapt continually. It involves recognizing that our choices will always have consequences and striving to make them as positive and meaningful as possible.

Footnotes

1. "The Dark Side of Plant-Based Food - It's More About Money Than You May Think," CNBC, Dec 2019, https://www.cnbc.com/2019/12/31/the-dark-side-of-plant-based-food-its-more-about-money-than-you-may-think.html

2. "Why Inuit People Eat Lots of Fat and Few Vegetables," The Atlantic, Jan 2016, https://www.theatlantic.com/health/archive/2016/01/the-inuit-paradox/423366/

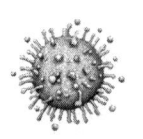

The Vegan Virus

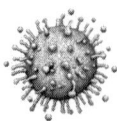

Ancestral Agricultural Wisdom

There is a tendency to look forward to innovation in the contemporary dialogue about diets and sustainability. Yet, the most profound wisdom often lies in gazing backward into the depths of ancestral knowledge. This chapter is a journey into the past, a study of traditional agricultural practices that our ancestors utilized to create a symbiotic relationship with nature. It is an exploration of ancient wisdom, a treasure trove of sustainable and ethical farming techniques that have been overshadowed by industrial advancements but are now more relevant than ever.

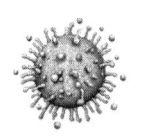

For millennia, human societies have thrived on agriculture that respected the limits and bounty of the natural world. Our ancestors were keen observers of ecosystems. They knew the patterns of the land, the seasons' cycles, and the animals' behaviors. They strove to balance productivity with ecosystem health, understanding the interdependence of all life forms[1]. This deep understanding of nature informed their farming practices, which were inherently sustainable and ethical.

Indigenous cultures worldwide have long practiced sustainable farming methods that preserved biodiversity, nurtured the soil, and promoted a harmonious coexistence with nature. For example, the Three Sisters farming system of Native Americans—an intercropping system of corn, beans, and squash—demonstrates an intricate understanding of plant synergies[2]. They created rich, fertile soils known as terra preta, using a combination of charcoal, bone, and manure. This enhanced the land's productivity and sequester carbon, a practice praised today for its environmental benefits.

In the meticulously designed terraced fields of Asia, innovative systems to cultivate rice alongside fish and ducks were developed[3]. These practices not only controlled pests but also fertilized the crops naturally. These paddies were more than mere food sources; they constituted ecosystems teeming with life, fostering vast biodiversity.

African shifting cultivation systems, often inaccurately perceived as primitive, essentially embodied the principles of regenerative agriculture[4]. They allowed for the land's recovery and preservation of fertility over time. Crop rotation and intercropping were not recent innovations but revered traditions that curtailed soil depletion and mitigated the spread of pests and diseases.

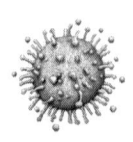

The Middle East, recognized as the cradle of agriculture, conceived ingenious irrigation techniques such as qanats to supply water to arid landscapes without exhausting the underground aquifers[5]. These ancient systems distributed water sustainably, ensuring life could prosper even under the most severe conditions.

These practices were not only sustainable but also ethical. They reflected a philosophy that saw humans as caretakers of the earth, not conquerors. Animals were integral to these systems, treated with respect, and provided a life that allowed them to fulfill their natural behaviors. This is in stark contrast to the often-criticized factory farming methods of today.

The wisdom of these traditional agricultural methods must be considered. They offer invaluable insights into how we can reshape modern agriculture into a truly sustainable and ethical form. By studying and understanding these practices, we can glean lessons that can be adapted and applied to our current context.
This ancestral wisdom also challenges the modern vegan perspective that animal farming is inherently cruel and environmentally destructive. It shows us that there is a way to include animals in our agricultural systems that is both compassionate and beneficial to the environment. It is not the presence of animals in farming that is the issue but the manner in which they are raised and integrated into the agricultural system.

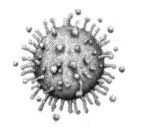

As we look to the future of our food systems, it is imperative that we embrace the lessons of the past. Ancestral agricultural wisdom can guide us in creating a model of agriculture that is not only productive but also nourishes the land, protects biodiversity, and respects all forms of life. It calls us to a more thoughtful way of interacting with our environment, one that honors the symbiotic relationship between the land, the plants, the animals, and the humans who tend them.

Footnotes

1. "Traditional Farming: An Overview," National Geographic, https://www.nationalgeographic.org/encyclopedia/traditional-farming/
2. "Three Sisters: The Original Sustainable Agriculture," USDA, https://www.usda.gov/media/blog/2016/08/10/three-sisters-original-sustainable-agriculture
3. "Rice-Fish Culture in China," International Rice Research Institute, https://www.irri.org/publications/irrn/rice-fish-culture-china
4. "Shifting Cultivation and Environmental Change: Indigenous People, Agriculture and Forest Conservation," Malcolm F. Cairns, 2015, https://books.google.com/books?id=1LuLBgAAQBAJ&printsec=frontcover#v=onepage&q&f=false
5. "Qanat, an Ancient Invention for Water Management in Iran," UNESCO, http://www.unesco.org/new/en/natural-sciences/environment/water/wwap/facts-and-figures/all-facts-wwdr3/fact-11-qanat/

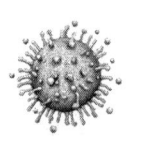

The Vegan Virus

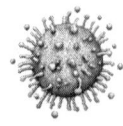

The Regenerative Future

As we have traversed the rich history of ancestral agricultural wisdom, it becomes evident that the future of sustainable and ethical farming may indeed echo the past, reframed for the present. In this chapter, we explore regenerative farming, a system of agriculture that is gaining recognition as a beacon of hope for the restoration of our ecosystems, the revitalization of our soils, and the reconnection of our communities to the land that sustains them.

Regenerative farming is more than a set of practices; it is a philosophy that seeks to rehabilitate and enhance the farm's entire ecosystem. It is an agriculture that works in harmony with nature, rather than against it. The ethos underlying regenerative farming is renewal, resilience, and respect for the intricate web of life.

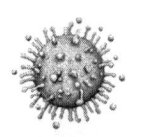

At its core, regenerative farming champions the following principles:

1) Soil Health: Regenerative farming is founded on the understanding that healthy soil is the bedrock of a healthy ecosystem. Practices such as no-till farming, cover cropping, and compost application help build organic matter, fostering a thriving community of microorganisms essential for nutrient cycling and soil structure.

2) Water Management: Efficient water use and the enhancement of natural water cycles are critical. Regenerative farmers work to increase water infiltration and retention in soils, reducing the need for irrigation and protecting water sources from contamination.

3) Biodiversity: Diverse ecosystems are resilient ecosystems. Regenerative agriculture encourages the cultivation of a variety of crops and the integration of livestock, creating a complex habitat for a wide range of species and reducing vulnerability to pests and diseases.

4) Integration of Livestock: Animals play a crucial role in regenerative systems, just as in natural ecosystems. Appropriately managed livestock can help cycle nutrients, control weeds, and pests, and improve soil health through natural behaviors.

5) Carbon Sequestration: By enhancing soil health and biomass through agroforestry and silvopasture, regenerative farming captures atmospheric carbon dioxide, contributing to climate change mitigation.

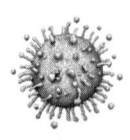

6) Farmer and Community Well-being: Regenerative agriculture recognizes that the well-being of the farmer and the community is inseparable from the health of the land. It seeks to strengthen local economies, ensure food security, and reconnect people with the natural world.

These principles are not prescriptive but adaptive; they can be tailored to the unique challenges and opportunities of each farm, region, and community.

Practices vary widely in regenerative agriculture but share a common goal: to create autonomous and self-renewing systems. Crop diversity and rotation break pest and disease cycles while enhancing the nutritional balance of the land. When integrated with crop production, livestock can graze on cover crops and pasture, turning waste into a valuable resource. Agroforestry, the incorporation of trees into farming systems, provides shelter for crops and animals, habitats for wildlife, and additional sources of income.

The regenerative ethos is also about the big picture. It's a recognition that agriculture doesn't exist in a vacuum. It's part of a larger ecological and social fabric. It's about looking beyond the borders of the farm to the surrounding landscapes and communities and seeing how they can all fit together in a mutually beneficial way.

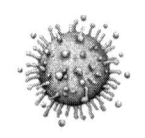

A regenerative future is not returning to the past or rejecting modern technology or innovation. It is, instead, a forward-looking integration of traditional wisdom with contemporary understanding. It is a path that honors the legacy of our ancestors while forging a sustainable legacy for the generations to come. It is a testament to the fact that the most advanced technologies and the most profound wisdom may be those that enable us to live as nature intended – interconnected, respectful, and regenerative.

Timboslice

The Vegan Virus

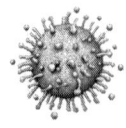

How Regenerative Agriculture Works

We've traversed the philosophical foundations and historical precedents that underpin regenerative farming[1]. Now, we will delve into the practical mechanics of how regenerative agriculture rejuvenates the land and serves as a potent antidote to some of our most pressing environmental issues: soil degradation, loss of biodiversity, and climate change[2].

Soil degradation poses a silent crisis threatening the very foundation of our food systems[3]. Regenerative farming confronts this issue head-on by prioritizing soil health as the linchpin of its practice[4]. Unlike conventional agriculture, which often leans on chemical inputs and heavy tillage disrupting soil biology and structure, regenerative farming practices are designed to mirror natural processes[5].

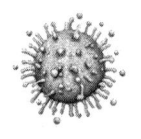

No-Till Farming: Spearheading the movement is no-till farming, a method abstaining from turning over the soil[6]. This practice preserves soil structure, safeguards the habitat of soil microorganisms, and curbs erosion. The lack of disturbance allows fungal networks to thrive, which is crucial for nutrient cycling and carbon storage[7].

Cover Cropping: Another essential practice is the utilization of cover crops—plants grown not for harvest but to shield the soil[8]. These can be legumes, grasses, or other plants that guard against erosion, suppress weeds, boost soil fertility, and enhance moisture retention. Cover crops are often used in rotation with cash crops to ensure that soil is never left bare, protecting against degradation[9].

Composting and Green Manures: The application of compost and green manures—plants plowed back into the soil to augment their organic matter—replenishes nutrients without synthetic fertilizers[10]. This feeds the soil and sequesters carbon, as composted plant material stores carbon that would otherwise be released into the atmosphere[11].

Integrated Pest Management (IPM): Regenerative farming also employs IPM strategies, utilizing a variety of biological, mechanical, and cultural techniques for pest control, reducing the need for chemical pesticides[12]. This approach fosters a balanced ecosystem where natural predators control harmful pests[13].

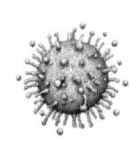

Agroforestry and Silvopasture: By incorporating trees and shrubs into farming systems (agroforestry) and merging forestry with grazing (silvopasture), regenerative agriculture fosters habitats for diverse species, augments the resilience of the land to climate extremes, and sequesters carbon in vegetation and soils[14].

By weaving these practices into the fabric of agriculture, regenerative farmers create a tapestry of benefits extending beyond their fields' boundaries. Soil health is the linchpin that holds this system together. Healthy soils are alive with microorganisms that break down organic matter, fix nitrogen and store carbon. They form the foundation of a stable ecosystem, supporting plant health and increasing resilience to pests and disease.

The loss of biodiversity is another symptom of ailing agricultural systems. Regenerative farming reverses this trend by promoting a diversity of plant and animal life within agricultural systems. This diversity is not only intrinsically valuable but also serves practical purposes. Different species of plants and animals fulfill various roles in the ecosystem, from pollination and pest control to nutrient cycling and soil aeration. By fostering this diversity, regenerative farms become more resilient and less dependent on external inputs.

Lastly, the shadow of climate change looms large over modern agriculture. Regenerative farming practices offer a beacon of hope. By enhancing soil carbon storage, these practices turn farms into carbon sinks, helping to offset greenhouse gas emissions. Moreover, the improvement of soil health leads to excellent water retention, which means regenerative farms are better equipped to withstand the extreme weather events that climate change brings.

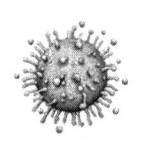

Regenerative farming is more than a romantic vision; it is a concrete methodology with the potential to transform our relationship with the land. It is an actionable plan for a future where agriculture contributes to the solution of our environmental crises, rather than perpetuating them. It is, ultimately, a pathway toward a more harmonious and sustainable coexistence with the Earth.

Footnotes
1. "Regenerative Agriculture: Principles, Pioneers + Does It Really Work?" by Emma Loewe, Mindbodygreen, https://www.mindbodygreen.com/articles/what-is-regenerative-agriculture
2. "Regenerative Agriculture: Farming to Improve Soil Health and Sequester Carbon," by Stephanie Anderson, National Geographic, https://www.nationalgeographic.com/environment/article/regenerative-agriculture-farming-soil-health-carbon-sequestration
3. "Soil degradation: A problem undermining human well-being," United Nations Environment Programme, https://www.unep.org/news-and-stories/story/soil-degradation-problem-undermining-human-well-being
4. "Regenerative Agriculture and Soil Health," Rodale Institute, https://rodaleinstitute.org/science/topics/soil-health/
5. "The Promise of Regenerative Agriculture," by Renee Cho, State of the Planet, Columbia University Earth Institute, https://blogs.ei.columbia.edu/2020/04/24/promise-regenerative-agriculture/
6. "No-Till Farming Pros and Cons," by Bethany Hayes, Urban Farming HQ, https://www.urbanfarmhq.com/no-till-farming-pros-cons/

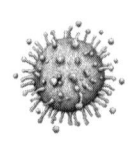

7. "No-Till: How Farmers Are Saving the Soil by Parking Their Plows," by Dan Charles, NPR, https://www.npr.org/sections/thesalt/2016/08/13/489982071/no-till-farmers-plant-seeds-without-plowing-to-save-soil

8. "Cover Crops and Soil Health," USDA Natural Resources Conservation Service, https://www.nrcs.usda.gov/wps/portal/nrcs/detailfull/soils/health/mgnt/?cid=nrcs142p2_053868

9. "Using Cover Crops in Your Farm Rotation," Cornell University, https://smallfarms.cornell.edu/2016/10/using-cover-crops-in-your-farm-rotation/

10. "Composting for Organic Farming," University of Maryland Extension, https://extension.umd.edu/resource/composting-organic-farming

11. "Carbon Sequestration in Soils," by Rattan Lal, Journal of Soil and Water Conservation, https://www.jswconline.org/content/57/6/464.short

12. "Integrated Pest Management (IPM) Principles," EPA, https://www.epa.gov/safepestcontrol/integrated-pest-management-ipm-principles

13. "Biological Control and Natural Enemies," University of California Statewide IPM Program, http://ipm.ucanr.edu/PMG/PESTNOTES/pn74140.html

14. "Agroforestry and Silvopasture in Regenerative Agriculture," Savory Institute, https://savory.global/holistic-management/agroforestry-silvopasture-regenerative-agriculture/

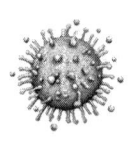

The Vegan Virus

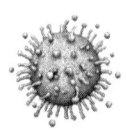

Regenerative Nutrition

In the realm of sustainable agriculture, a crucial yet often overlooked aspect is the nutritional quality of the produce. Regenerative Nutrition focuses on the richness and wholesomeness of foods grown on regenerative farms, offering a compelling argument for choosing these foods regardless of one's dietary orientation. Whether vegan, vegetarian, or omnivorous, the emphasis is clear: foods from regenerative sources are superior in nourishment and pivotal for healthier lifestyles.

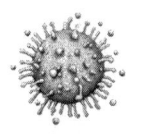

At the core of regenerative agriculture is the health of the soil[1]. Rich, vibrant soils, abundant in organic matter and bustling with microbial life, are not just good for the planet; they are the foundation of nutrient-dense crops. Studies have consistently shown that plants nurtured in these soils boast higher levels of essential nutrients – vitamins, minerals, and antioxidants[2] – surpassing those grown in the depleted soils of conventional agriculture. The connection between the vitality of the earth and the quality of the produce it yields is inextricable and profound.

This principle extends beyond plant-based foods to encompass animal products as well. Animals raised on regenerative farms, grazing on lush, diverse pastures, yield meat, dairy, and nutritionally superior eggs[3]. These products are often richer in omega-3 fatty acids, conjugated linoleic acid (CLA), and various vitamins[4]. The enhanced nutritional profile directly results from the animals' diet and their healthful environments, which starkly contrasts the conditions in conventional animal farming.

Moreover, regenerative farms promote a diversity of crops and livestock, a stark departure from the monocultures characterizing much of modern agriculture[5]. This biodiversity is not just beneficial for the environment; it encourages a more varied human diet. Embracing various foods is critical to achieving a balanced and nutritionally complete diet. Regenerative farming, with its array of produce and animal products, naturally aligns with this principle of dietary diversity, offering a spectrum of nutrients essential for human health[6].

This approach to farming has significant implications for global nutrition, particularly in combating the widespread issue of micronutrient deficiencies, often referred to as 'hidden hunger.' By enhancing the nutrient density of plant- and animal-based foods, regenerative farming practices emerge as powerful allies in the fight against global nutritional challenges[7].

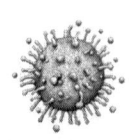

Accessibility to these nutrient-rich foods is increasing thanks to a growing network of farmers' markets, community-supported agriculture (CSA) programs, and online platforms[8]. Even in conventional shopping venues, there's a rising presence of products sourced from regenerative agriculture. Consumers are now more empowered to make choices that enrich their diets and contribute to the planet's healing[9].

Regenerative nutrition transcends the act of eating. It represents a holistic approach to nourishing the body and the earth. People across various dietary spectrums can partake in nourishment that supports and sustains the planet's health by opting for foods from regenerative sources. It's a choice that intertwines dietary preferences with environmental responsibility, highlighting that where our food comes from is as crucial as the food itself. Regenerative nutrition is not just a pathway to healthier eating; it's a step towards a more vibrant and sustainable world.

Footnotes

1. "Regenerative Agriculture Part 4: The Benefits," NRDC, https://www.nrdc.org/bio/arohi-sharma/regenerative-agriculture-part-4-benefits

2. "Regenerative Agriculture," Chesapeake Bay Foundation, https://www.cbf.org/issues/agriculture/regenerative-agriculture.html

3. "Why Regenerative Agriculture?," Regeneration International, https://regenerationinternational.org/why-regenerative-agriculture/

4. "5 benefits of regenerative agriculture – and 5 ways to scale it," World Economic Forum, https://www.weforum.org/agenda/2023/01/5-ways-to-scale-regenerative-agriculture-davos23/

5. "Principles and benefits of regenerative agriculture," Enel, https://www.enel.com/company/stories/articles/2022/11/regenerative-agriculture

6. "What is Regenerative Agriculture and How Does it Benefit...," Climate Farmers, https://www.climatefarmers.org/blog/what-is-regenerative-agriculture-and-how-does-it-benefit-your-farm/

7. "5 Benefits of Regenerative Agriculture – and 5 Ways to...," Agribusiness Global, https://www.agribusinessglobal.com/sustainability/5-benefits-of-regenerative-agriculture-and-5-ways-to-scale-it/

8. "Top 5 Benefits Of Regenerative Agriculture [INFOGRAPHIC]," Holganix, https://www.holganix.com/blog/top-5-benefits-of-regenerative-agriculture-infographic

9. "The Case for Regenerative Agriculture in Germany—and...," BCG, https://www.bcg.com/publications/2023/regenerative-agriculture-benefits-germany-beyond

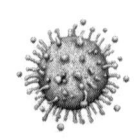

Timboslice

The Vegan Virus

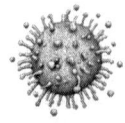

Solving Scalability

The challenge of feeding a burgeoning global population is one of the most pressing issues facing humanity[1]. Critics of regenerative agriculture often cite scalability as a stumbling block, arguing that while these practices are ideal for small-scale operations, they must be more effectively upscaled to meet global food demands[2]. This chapter confronts this skepticism head-on, unpacking how regenerative agriculture can scale up to feed the world and sustainably[3].

To start with, we must debunk the myth that industrial agriculture is the only way to feed the world[4]. This notion is based on a paradigm that equates sheer yield with food security, disregarding distribution, waste, nutritional value, and environmental impact[5]. Regenerative agriculture offers a more holistic approach, aiming not just to produce large quantities of food but to do so in a way that preserves the Earth's resources for future generations[6].

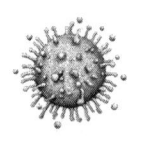

Diversification Over Monoculture: One of the core tenets of regenerative agriculture is diversification[7]. Unlike monocultures, vulnerable to pests, diseases, and climate vagaries, diverse cropping systems are resilient and productive[8]. By cultivating a variety of crops and integrating livestock, regenerative farms can produce a wide array of foodstuffs, enhancing overall yield and resilience[9].

Localized Food Systems: Scalability does not necessarily mean centralization[10]. A network of smaller, diversified, interconnected regenerative farms can create a robust food system. Localized production reduces transportation costs and carbon footprints and increases the freshness and nutritional value of food[11]. By investing in local food systems, we can create a scalable yet decentralized model tailored to the specific needs and capacities of different regions[12].

Technology and Innovation: Modern technology is not antithetical to regenerative farming but can be harnessed to augment it[13]. Innovations in precision agriculture, such as drones and sensors, can optimize resource use and crop planning[14]. Permaculture and agroecological design advances can be applied on larger scales to maximize efficiency and productivity[15].

Policy Support and Investment: Scaling up regenerative agriculture requires policy support and investment[16]. Governments and financial institutions have a crucial role in incentivizing regenerative practices[17]. Subsidies, grants, and loan programs directed toward regenerative agriculture can drive a transition on a larger scale[18].

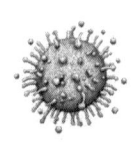

Additionally, research into regenerative techniques must be funded to refine and adapt practices for different scales and contexts[19].

Education and Knowledge Sharing: Knowledge is a crucial driver of chang[20]. Education programs for farmers and consumers about the benefits of regenerative agriculture can lead to increased adoption[21]. Peer-to-peer networks and cooperative extensions can facilitate the sharing best practices and innovations, enabling farmers to learn and adapt quickly[22].

Market Demand: Consumer demand can be a powerful catalyst for change[23]. As more consumers request products from regenerative systems, the market will respond. Certification programs for regeneratively grown products can help consumers make informed choices, encouraging more farmers to adopt regenerative practices[24].

Addressing Food Waste: A significant portion of the food produced globally is wasted[25]. We can make more food available without increasing production by addressing inefficiencies in the food system and improving storage, processing, and distribution. Regenerative agriculture, with its emphasis on local systems, can contribute to these solutions by shortening the supply chain.

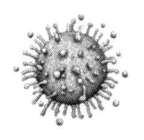

The narrative that regenerative agriculture is not scalable is often perpetuated by those who benefit from the status quo. However, with the proper support, innovation, and community engagement, regenerative agriculture can indeed be scaled to meet the needs of a growing population. It can transform from a patchwork of small success stories into a global movement that ensures food security, ecological health, and equitable economic development. The task is undoubtedly complex, but the bright examples of regenerative success and the inexhaustible human capacity for adaptation and innovation illuminate the path.

Footnotes

1. "World population projected to reach 9.8 billion in 2050, and 11.2 billion in 2100," United Nations Department of Economic and Social Affairs, https://www.un.org/development/desa/en/news/population/world-population-prospects-2017.html

2. "Can Regenerative Agriculture Scale Up?" by Renee Cho, State of the Planet, Columbia University Earth Institute, https://blogs.ei.columbia.edu/2021/02/02/regenerative-agriculture-scale-up/

3. "Regenerative Agriculture Can Feed the World – Without Trashing It," by John Roulac, Regeneration International, https://regenerationinternational.org/2018/06/18/regenerative-agriculture-can-feed-the-world-without-trashing-it/

4. "Debunking the myth that only industrial ag can 'feed the world'," by Anna Lappé, The Guardian, https://www.theguardian.com/commentisfree/2016/oct/15/agricultural-giant-threatens-us-food-supply

5. "Feeding the world: Agriculture, nutrition and ecological sustainability," by David Tilman and Michael Clark, Science, https://science.sciencemag.org/content/362/6416/705

6. "Regenerative Agriculture: Farming to Improve Soil Health and Sequester Carbon," by Stephanie Anderson, National Geographic, https://www.nationalgeographic.com/environment/article/regenerative-agriculture-farming-soil-health-carbon-sequestration

7. "Diversity: A Key Aspect of 21st Century Agriculture," by Katherine Stanley, Manitoba Cooperator, https://www.manitobacooperator.ca/crops/diversity-a-key-aspect-of-21st-century-agriculture/

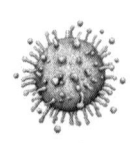

8. "Crop Diversification: An Important Strategy for Climate Change Adaptation," by B Venkateswarlu, Indian Journal of Agronomy, https://www.researchgate.net/publication/282645919_Crop_diversification_An_important_strategy_for_climate_change_adaptation

9. "Integrating Livestock into Cropping Systems Can Be a Sustainable Strategy to Improve Soil Health and Farm Resilience," USDA, https://www.ars.usda.gov/news-events/news/research-news/2020/integrating-livestock-into-cropping-systems-can-be-a-sustainable-strategy-to-improve-soil-health-and-farm-resilience/

10. "Local Food Systems: Concepts, Impacts, and Issues," by Steve Martinez, USDA, https://www.ers.usda.gov/webdocs/publications/46393/7054_err97_1_.pdf?v=42265

11. "The impact of food supply chain characteristics on food security: An empirical study of Ghanaian fresh produce supply chain," by Jing Zhao, British Food Journal, https://www.emerald.com/insight/content/doi/10.1108/BFJ-11-2017-0642/full/html

12. "Building Local and Regional Food Systems," National Sustainable Agriculture Coalition, http://sustainableagriculture.net/publications/grassrootsguide/local-food-systems/

13. "Farm Tech: 5 AgTech Innovations That Combine Farming and Technology," by Loukia Papadopoulos, Interesting Engineering, https://interestingengineering.com/farm-tech-5-agtech-innovations-that-combine-farming-and-technology

14. "Transforming Agriculture Through Technology," by Laura Kahn, Bulletin of the Atomic Scientists, https://thebulletin.org/2018/10/transforming-agriculture-through-technology/

15. "Agroecology Can Help Fix Our Broken Food System. Here's How," by Elizabeth Henderson, Civil Eats, https://civileats.com/2018/06/26/agroecology-can-help-fix-our-broken-food-system-heres-how/

16. "Regenerative Agriculture and the Soil Carbon Solution," by Richard Teague et al., Green Money Journal, https://greenmoney.com/regenerative-agriculture-and-the-soil-carbon-solution/

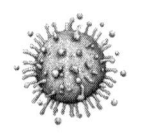

17. "Investing in Regenerative Agriculture: Making Finance Serve Nature," by Thomas Lorber, The Beam, https://the-beam.com/climate-action/investing-in-regenerative-agriculture-making-finance-serve-nature/
18. "How to Transition to Regenerative Farming Using Government Grants," by Ben Hartman, Rodale Institute, https://rodaleinstitute.org/blog/how-to-transition-to-regenerative-farming-using-government-grants/
19. "Scaling up regenerative agriculture: strategies, best practices, and barriers," by Courtney White, Resilience, https://www.resilience.org/stories/2014-10-08/scaling-up-regenerative-agriculture-strategies-best-practices-and-barriers/
20. "Education for Sustainable Development Goals: Learning Objectives," UNESCO, https://unesdoc.unesco.org/ark:/48223/pf0000247444
21. "Education and Training," Regenerative Agriculture Alliance, https://regenag.co/education-training/
22. "Peer-to-peer learning for farmers," by Thea Whitman, Cornell University, https://smallfarms.cornell.edu/2016/04/peer-to-peer-learning-for-farmers/
23. "Consumer Demand for Regenerative Food & Farming," by Aaron Kinsman, Rodale Institute, https://rodaleinstitute.org/blog/consumer-demand-for-regenerative-food-farming/
24. "Certified Regenerative," Regenerative Organic Alliance, https://regenorganic.org/certified-regenerative/
25. "Global food losses and food waste," Food and Agriculture Organization of the United Nations, http://www.fao.org/

Timboslice

The Vegan Virus

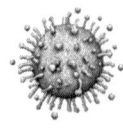

Transition Agriculture

The vision of regenerative agriculture feeding the world is compelling, but the path from our current state to that sustainable future is laden with challenges. This chapter addresses the transitional strategies that could bridge the gap between conventional agriculture and regenerative practices on a global scale. It is about converting potential into reality, managing the 'how' of the transformation, and ensuring that this transition is just, equitable, and feasible for farmers and communities worldwide.

Transitioning Existing Farms: The shift begins with the gradual transition of existing farms. This requires a step-by-step approach, where farmers adopt regenerative practices incrementally. Support in the form of education, training, and financial incentives can ease this transition, making it less daunting. A key component is developing a transition plan that considers the unique circumstances of each farm, ensuring that changes are economically and ecologically sustainable.

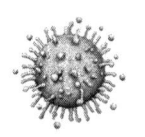

Financial Mechanisms and Risk Management: Financial barriers often prevent farmers from adopting new practices. To mitigate this, innovative financial mechanisms such as crop insurance for regenerative techniques, low-interest loans for transitioning farms, and investment in regenerative agriculture start-ups can play a crucial role. These mechanisms must be designed to manage the risks associated with transitioning, providing a safety net that encourages farmers to undertake this change.

Policy Frameworks: Governments can accelerate the transition by implementing policy frameworks that favor regenerative practices. This could include revising agricultural subsidies, supporting soil health initiatives, and establishing carbon credit markets where farmers are rewarded for sequestering carbon. Policies must also be crafted to protect smallholder farmers and keep them in the transition.

Scalable Models of Success: To illustrate the feasibility of transition, scalable models of regenerative farming that have proven successful must be highlighted and analyzed. These models serve as blueprints that can be adapted and replicated, demonstrating to policymakers, farmers, and the global community that regenerative agriculture can work on a large scale.

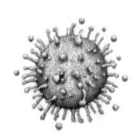

Technology and Data: Leveraging technology can facilitate the transition by providing farmers with the tools and data they need to implement regenerative practices effectively. This includes remote sensing for soil health monitoring, blockchain for traceability in supply chains, and platforms for sharing knowledge and resources among the regenerative farming community.

Market Development and Consumer Awareness: Developing markets for regeneratively produced goods is crucial. This involves creating consumer awareness of the benefits of regenerative products and establishing supply chains and marketplaces that can handle these goods. Certification schemes can assure consumers and create premium market segments.

Collaboration and Community Involvement: Transitioning to regenerative agriculture is a collective effort. It requires collaboration between farmers, agribusinesses, non-profits, governments, and communities. Establishing community-led initiatives can empower local stakeholders and ensure that the transition reflects the needs and values of the people it affects.

Global Partnerships: Finally, global partnerships are essential. Climate change and food security are global challenges that require a united front. International collaborations can support knowledge exchange, align global policies, and mobilize resources to support the transition to regenerative practices worldwide.

The transition to regenerative agriculture is a challenging fix. It is a profound transformation of the way we interact with our planet's resources. It is a call to action for all sectors of society to play a role in this vital change, ensuring that the future of agriculture heals the planet while nourishing its inhabitants.

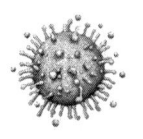

The Vegan Virus

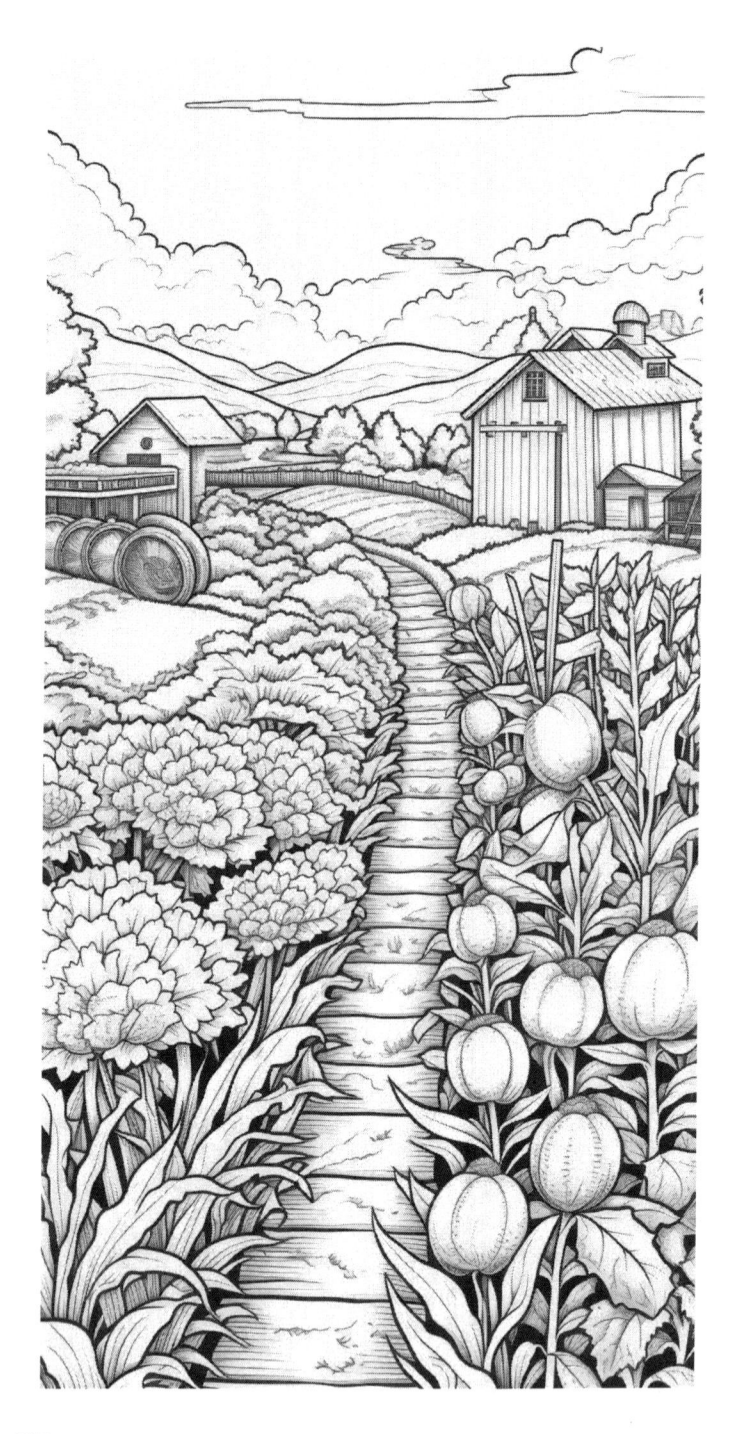

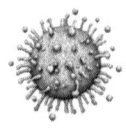

Cultivating Consumer Consciousness and Demand

The shift toward regenerative agriculture hinges not just on transforming farming practices but also on evolving consumer behavior and demand. Consumers wield immense power in the agricultural market; their choices can significantly influence farming practices globally. Recognizing this, the chapter discusses the importance of consumer awareness and its impact on promoting regenerative agriculture.

Education plays a crucial role in molding consumer choices. Most of the population must be aware of the environmental and social impacts of their food choices. Effective educational campaigns, transparent labeling initiatives, and increased media coverage can help bridge this knowledge gap. They can inform consumers about the benefits of regenerative agriculture, both environmentally and socially, leading to more conscientious purchasing decisions.

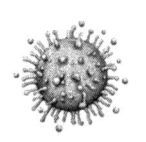

However, consumer education must be complemented by transparency in the food supply chain. Technologies like blockchain can offer this transparency, providing a clear view of the journey of food from farm to table. This level of clarity can reinforce consumer trust in regeneratively produced products, encouraging their wider acceptance.

Addressing the cost and accessibility of products from regenerative farming is another crucial aspect. While such products are often perceived as more expensive, making them accessible and affordable is critical to widespread consumer adoption. Strategies like achieving economies of scale in regenerative farming, introducing governmental subsidies, and encouraging community-supported agriculture can help.

Changing entrenched consumer habits requires a strategic approach. Insights from successful case studies where shifts in consumer behavior have supported more sustainable practices can offer valuable lessons. The influence of marketing, social trends, and cultural shifts significantly shape consumer preferences towards sustainability.

The trend towards organic products has already shown how consumer demand can drive change in agricultural practices. A similar growing demand for regenerative products has the potential to set a new market trend, supporting environmental and social well-being.

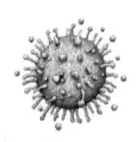

Reconnecting consumers with their local food systems is fundamental to this transition. Engagement in local food movements and community initiatives can foster a deeper appreciation of regenerative farming practices. This grassroots-level involvement can strengthen local markets for regenerative products, providing critical support for the broader transition.

In essence, the path to a sustainable future in agriculture is significantly influenced by consumer behavior. Awareness, transparency, and active engagement are critical elements in driving the demand that can reshape the agricultural landscape, underscoring the power of consumers in supporting a more sustainable and regenerative world.

The Vegan Virus

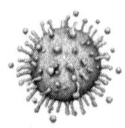

Future Farming

In envisioning the future of agriculture, it becomes increasingly clear that integrating emerging high-tech farming techniques with regenerative farming practices can create a powerful synergy. The latest advancements in technology can enhance and amplify the principles of regenerative agriculture, paving the way for a future that is both technologically advanced and deeply rooted in sustainable practices.

Precision Agriculture: Enhancing Efficiency and Sustainability: Precision agriculture, utilizing GPS, data analytics, and IoT sensors, can revolutionize regenerative farming[1]. This technology enables farmers to monitor and optimize the health of their soil and plants with unparalleled precision. By applying water, nutrients, and organic pesticides exactly where and when needed, farmers can reduce waste and environmental impact, preserving regenerative farming principles while enhancing productivity.

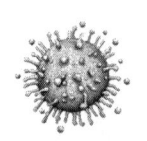

Drone Technology: A Bird's-Eye View for Better Farm Management: Drones are increasingly becoming indispensable in futuristic farming landscapes[2]. In regenerative agriculture, drones offer numerous uses, including monitoring crop health, assessing soil conditions, and even planting seeds. They provide a unique vantage point, allowing farmers to make informed decisions that align with regenerative principles, such as identifying areas that need more organic matter or detecting early signs of pest infestations.

AI and Machine Learning: Predictive Analytics for Smarter Farming: Artificial Intelligence (AI) and machine learning hold significant potential in predicting and managing complex variables in farming[3]. These technologies can analyze data from various sources like weather patterns, soil conditions, and crop health to provide insights for better crop management. They can predict outcomes, suggest optimal crop rotations, and inform decisions that enhance the regenerative capacity of the land.

Robotics: Automating Tasks While Protecting the Land: Robotics in agriculture, from automated tractors to robotic harvesters, can perform repetitive tasks with precision and efficiency[4]. In a regenerative farming context, these machines can minimize soil compaction and disturbance, protecting the soil structure and microbiome. Robots can also assist in weeding and harvesting, reducing the need for herbicides and ensuring crops are picked at their nutritional peak.

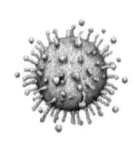

Vertical Farming and Controlled Environment Agriculture: While regenerative farming is often linked with open fields, vertical farming and Controlled Environment Agriculture (CEA) in urban settings align with its principles by optimizing space and resources[5]. These systems can use hydroponics and aeroponics to grow crops with minimal water and no soil erosion. Powered by renewable energy, they present an exciting, sustainable model for producing food closer to where it's consumed, reducing transportation emissions and resource use.

Blockchain for Transparency and Traceability: Blockchain technology can provide unparalleled transparency in the agricultural supply chain[6]. By securely tracking the journey of food from farm to table, blockchain ensures that regenerative practices used in growing and harvesting crops are visible and verifiable by consumers. Such transparency builds trust and can increase consumer demand for regeneratively grown products.

Integrating Traditional Knowledge with Modern Tech: A crucial aspect of future farming is the integration of traditional agricultural knowledge with modern technology[7]. This blend respects and utilizes centuries-old practices that have sustained lands and communities while enhancing them with today's technological capabilities.

1. "The Environmental Benefits of Precision Agriculture," AEM, https://www.aem.org/news/the-environmental-benefits-of-precision-agriculture-quantified

2. "Precision Farming: 7 Ways it Benefits Your Farm," FarmersEdge, https://farmersedge.ca/precision-farming-7-ways-it-benefits-your-farm/

3. "What is precision agriculture and what are the benefits of AI," Quora, https://www.quora.com/What-is-precision-agriculture-and-what-are-the-benefits-of-AI-in-this

4. "Advantages and role of precision agriculture technology," Geopard.tech, https://geopard.tech/blog/what-is-precision-farming/

5. "Precision Agriculture: Advantages, Limitations, and Future Directions," LinkedIn, https://www.linkedin.com/advice/1/how-can-precision-agriculture-integrate-other-emerging

6. "Blockchain: an accelerator for women and agribusiness," World Bank Blogs, https://blogs.worldbank.org/nasikiliza/blockchain-accelerator-women-and-agribusiness

7. "Traditional Knowledge & Indigenous Peoples," WIPO, https://www.wipo.int/pressroom/en/briefs/traditional_knowledge.html

Timboslice

The Vegan Virus

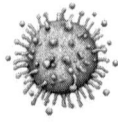

The Bright Future Ahead

As this book draws to a close, we stand at a crossroads, where the lessons learned and the insights gained throughout pave the way toward a future replete with hope and transformative potential. This journey, which began with a critical examination of veganism, has evolved into a much broader discourse on the profound connections between our dietary choices, the health of our planet, and the well-being of its inhabitants. At this pivotal juncture, we look ahead to a future where heightened awareness and proactive stewardship converge to redefine our relationship with the natural world.

This emerging future is characterized by a global shift in consciousness that transcends conventional dietary labels and penetrates the core of our understanding of food and sustainability. Individuals around the world are increasingly questioning not only what lies on their plates but also the origins and impacts of their food.

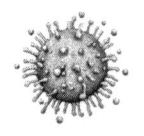

This goes beyond nutritional content or adherence to a particular diet; it represents a more profound awakening to the interconnectedness of our health with the vitality of the Earth. This growing awareness is dismantling long-held barriers, revealing a universal truth: the source and method of our food production are of paramount importance.

This awakening extends to recognizing the immense power inherent in every individual choice. Our daily decisions - what we eat, what we buy, and how we live - are no longer seen as mere personal preferences but as significant acts of environmental and ethical significance. We are, each one of us, custodians of the Earth, entrusted with the responsibility of nurturing and protecting this planet that sustains us. In this role, we are called not just to conserve but to actively restore and replenish the environment to embrace our role as shepherds of the land.

The shift we are witnessing today is not a fleeting trend but the genesis of a profound transformation in our societal and environmental interactions. This book serves as a testament to our incredible potential to effect meaningful change. We stand on the threshold of a new era that respects and cherishes the planet as profoundly as it does our health and prosperity.

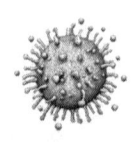

Looking forward, this vision of the future is imbued with optimism and actionable hope. The changes taking root around us are the embryonic stages of a significant transformation in our global food system and environmental stewardship. This transformation envisions a world where each person is empowered to make a difference, where our collective choices support and uplift farmers and producers committed to sustainable and ethical practices. It's a future where advocating for policies that promote environmental health and educating others about the importance of sustainable food sourcing are ingrained in our societal fabric.

In this envisioned future, the dialogue around food and agriculture is no longer polarized or confined to narrow definitions. Instead, it's a rich, inclusive conversation that acknowledges the diverse needs and capacities of ecosystems and communities across the globe. It's a future where the principles of regenerative agriculture, which have been a focal point of this book, become the norm rather than the exception. This approach to farming, harmonious with nature and respectful of all forms of life, becomes the foundation of a food system that is not only sustainable but also resilient and just.

Technology, often seen as a double-edged sword, plays a pivotal role in this future. Innovations in agricultural technology are harmonized with traditional, time-tested practices, creating a symbiosis that maximizes efficiency while maintaining ecological balance. Empowering with technology and information, consumers make choices that support this sustainable model, creating a demand that drives large-scale change in the agricultural sector.

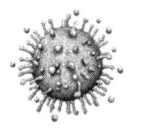

Education and community engagement are also critical drivers of this transformation. Schools, universities, and community programs emphasize the importance of sustainable living, creating a new environmentally conscious and proactive generation. Grassroots movements, bolstered by global collaboration, become a powerful force for change, influencing policy and corporate practices.

This bright future also sees a shift in dietary patterns. The focus is on quality and sustainability rather than adhering strictly to labels like 'vegan' or 'omnivore.' People choose foods not only for their health benefits but also for their environmental and ethical implications. The false dichotomy between different dietary preferences gives way to a more inclusive understanding that respects individual choices while emphasizing the collective responsibility towards the planet.

As this book concludes, it's with a call to action. This is a call to change our diets and our mindset about food, agriculture, and our relationship with the Earth. It's a call to embrace our role as stewards of the planet, to engage in thoughtful consumption, and to advocate for policies and practices that safeguard the health of our planet for current and future generations.

In this bright future, we envision a world where nourishing ourselves and caring for the planet are the same. A world where every meal, every choice, is a reflection of our respect for the Earth and all its inhabitants. "The Vegan Virus" started as a critique of a singular solution to our complex environmental and ethical challenges. It ends with a hopeful vision of a diverse, sustainable, and compassionate future that we all have the power to create.

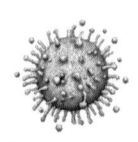

Timboslice

As always, keep crushing it, and I believe in You.

About the Author

Timboslice

Timboslice, a former professional baseball player, turned passionate advocate for nutrition, presents a compelling exploration of our food system in the "The Vegan Virus". His journey into the world of health and wellness began with a simple question: Where does our food come from? This inquiry unveiled a myriad of truths about food production and consumption, shaping his perspective and inspiring his writing.

In "The Vegan Virus", Timboslice combines his athletic discipline and keen interest in nutrition to challenge and inform readers about the impact of dietary choices on personal health and the environment. Beyond the field, he is an ardent software and AI developer, graphic designer, and entreprenuer.

Residing in Georgia, Timboslice continues to inspire and engage audiences with his groundbreaking insights and dedication to a healthier, more conscious world.

Linktree:
https://linktr.ee/Timboslice21x

Made in the USA
Columbia, SC
05 December 2023